Teacher's Assessment Handbook

D1514937

CONTENTS

Part 1

Introduction

Assessment—the process of gathering information to aid in the evaluation of students—is an important if somewhat nerve-racking topic in education today. More and more states are testing students' reading and writing achievement, and teachers are feeling the pressure to make sure that their students perform well.

Indeed, teachers are at the center of the kind of assessment that matters more—and that ultimately can affect large-scale proficiency test results: assessment that grows out of and affects day-to-day instruction. When teachers assess students' work, learning processes, and understanding—and plan instruction based on this assessment—student achievement increases. Further, when students are involved in their own assessment, setting goals and making decisions about their work, they become reflective, strategic learners.

The Teacher's Assessment Handbook presents a practical approach to creating an assessment-based literacy classroom. It presents a range of assessment types:

- assessment for initial screening, diagnosis, and instructional planning;
- ongoing informal assessment of reading, writing, and listening, speaking, and viewing;
- holistic and analytic evaluation of writing;
- formal assessment;
- assessment for meeting individual needs.

It also suggests strategies to help you prepare your students for standardized tests.

Perhaps most important, the handbook details, in both margin boxes and end-of-chapter charts, resources in HOUGHTON MIFFLIN READING that can help you modify instruction based on your ongoing informal assessment and periodic formal assessment.

Additional features include

- an Assessment Planning Guide;
- blackline masters for helpful checklists and forms;
- a resource bibliography of books, articles, and Internet sites.

Part 2

Assessment Resources in Houghton Mifflin Reading

Each Selection

- **Monitoring Student Progress** boxes throughout the Back to School Read Aloud selection in the *Teacher's Edition* help you informally assess students' use of reading strategies.

- **Monitoring Student Progress** at the end of each reading selection segment in the *Teacher's Edition* help you assess skills and make instructional decisions based on your assessment. These checks also appear in the Comprehension Skills, Phonics or Structural Analysis, High-Frequency Words, and Grammar Skills lessons; in each Reteaching lesson; and in each Leveled Reader lesson.

- **Student Self-Assessment** questions appear in the *Teacher's Edition* at the end of each main reading selection and at the end of each theme's Reading-Writing Workshop.

- **Portfolio Opportunity** reminders in the Writing Skills lessons and Reading-Writing Workshop in the *Teacher's Edition,* and on a variety of *Practice Book* pages, help you collect work samples covering a range of skills.

- **Comprehension Checks** for all reading selections are included in the *Practice Book* for each grade level.

- **Observation Checklists** in the *Teacher's Resource Blackline Masters* help you informally assess student progress by selection (Grades 2–6), by week (Grade 1), or by theme (K).

- **Selection Tests** for all main reading selections in a given grade level can be found in the *Teacher's Resource Blackline Masters.* These tests assess students' selection comprehension and vocabulary.

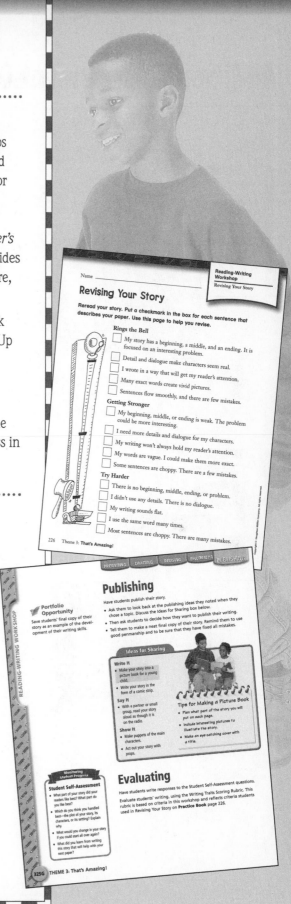

End of Theme

- **Check Your Progress** in the pupil book (Grades 2–6) helps students prepare for testing by comparing paired fiction and nonfiction selections, as they are often asked to do on major tests. **Taking Tests** (Grades 1.3–6) teaches strategies for answering the types of questions and prompts commonly found on local and state standardized tests. In your *Teacher's Edition,* **Monitoring Student Progress** (Grades 2–6) provides lessons and practice for connecting and comparing literature, test-taking strategies, and skill review.

- Oral **Reading Fluency** assessment guidelines in the Back to School section and in each Theme Assessment Wrap-Up help you take oral reading records and plan instruction based on the results.

- A **Differentiating Instruction** chart in each Theme Assessment Wrap-Up helps you modify instruction for the next theme based on your assessment of student progress in the current theme.

In the Reading-Writing Workshop

From Level 1.3 on, each theme in HOUGHTON MIFFLIN READING contains a Reading-Writing Workshop featuring a student writing model. Each workshop concludes with several assessment features.

- **Writing Traits Scoring Rubric** for holistic evaluation of writing that students produce in the workshop (See pages 40–59 in this handbook for six-point rubrics.)

- **Portfolio Opportunity** reminder

- **Student Self-Assessment** suggestions give questions students might use to evaluate their finished work and reflect on their writing experience

- **Revising Checklist** for each writing type to help students evaluate their papers as they revise

Additional Assessment Components

Instructional Planning and Placement

- The **Emerging Literacy Survey** (K–2), which assesses phonemic awareness, familiarity with print, and beginning reading and writing, helps identify children who need early intervention. It also allows you to identify and build on children's literacy strengths and to chart their progress over time.

- The **Lexia Quick Phonics Assessment CD-ROM** contains a total of twelve tests at three levels (K–1, 2, and 3–6) that identify students' strengths and weaknesses in phonics and decoding. It also recommends specific support on two phonics intervention CD-ROMs.

- The **Houghton Mifflin Phonics/Decoding Screening Test** helps you identify and plan instruction for students from the middle of Grade 1 through Grade 6 who lack basic phonics and decoding skills. You can also use the test to identify students who need phonics intervention and to develop small instructional groups for meeting individual needs.

- The **Houghton Mifflin Leveled Reading Passages Assessment Kit** helps you to measure the reading accuracy, rate, fluency, and comprehension of students in Grades K–6. It contains a set of carefully leveled passages that you can use throughout the year.

- The **Baseline Group Test** can be given at the beginning of the year to measure students' reading abilities and instructional needs. This test will help you plan instructional support for individual students.

Theme Tests

- The **Integrated Theme Tests** assess the skills and strategies taught in each theme. The tests use theme-related reading selections and evaluate reading strategies, reading and listening comprehension, phonemic awareness, phonics, word skills, writing, and language.

- The **Theme Skills Tests** assess students' grasp of the specific reading and language skills taught in each theme. These criterion-referenced tests can be used to customize whole-class or individual instruction and to prepare students for certain standardized assessments.

Benchmark Progress Tests

The **Benchmark Progress Tests** evaluate reading levels and writing levels of students in Grades 1–6 compared to a national sample. To monitor progress over time, you can give these tests at the beginning, middle, and end of the year.

Houghton Mifflin Reading Assessment on the Internet

The Internet home page for HOUGHTON MIFFLIN READING (http://www.eduplace.com/rdg/hmr) links you with additional up-to-date assessment resources:

- **theme-related activities** useful for instruction and informal assessment

- **professional papers by the authors** of HOUGHTON MIFFLIN READING, including an article on assessment

Internet
Tech Tip

Other Internet sites also contain useful assessment information. One excellent site is

- **Ericae.net,** a federally funded Educational Resources Information Center clearing-house on assessment, evaluation, and research information. URL: http://ericae.net

Part 3

Planning an Assessment-Based Literacy Classroom

Introduction

An assessment-based literacy classroom is one in which assessment is integrated with daily instructional activities. As students are engaged in instructional activities and experiences with literature, the teacher gathers information about students' literacy development. Essentially, assessment and instruction are all but indistinguishable—they occur concurrently, and each informs and influences the other.

Developing an Assessment-Based Instructional Plan

As you develop your classroom assessment plan, try to make it inseparable from your instructional plan. Doing so will enable you to assess students on the skills and strategies they have been taught. Also, with an ongoing assessment plan in place, you can monitor student progress throughout a grading period and adjust your instructional focus according to student needs. The first step is deciding where to begin.

Early in the year, acquaint yourself with your students—with their abilities and their instructional needs. You can accomplish this by

- conferencing with and observing the students;
- reviewing the previous year's work samples or teacher comments;
- assessing students informally;
- administering some formal assessment instruments (see Part 4, pages 10–17).

The next step is to set goals. Use the information you have gathered so far to establish a baseline, or starting point, for individual students and for the class as a whole. Then begin to set the learning goals, both short-term and long-term, that you want your students to attain.

When setting goals, consider not only the curriculum goals you have set for your classroom but also the goals in your state and district curriculum frameworks or guidelines.

ASSESSMENT AND INSTRUCTION

Assessment: Establishing a Baseline

Setting Goals

Establishing Criteria for Meeting Goals

Instructional Activities/Ongoing Informal Assessment

Modified Instructional Activities/Ongoing Informal Assessment

Periodic Formal Assessment

You may find these suggestions helpful as you develop classroom activities to meet your instructional goals.

- First, decide which indicators you will look for as evidence of students' success with each goal.
- Then list several activities through which students can demonstrate achievement of the goal indicators.
- Plan to use a variety of assessment activities so that students will have different opportunities to demonstrate what they have learned.
- Identify two or three methods for assessing each goal.

The chart below may help to clarify how to plan assessment for a given instructional goal.

Program Resources

The Learning More About Your Students and Planning for Instruction pages in the Back to School section of the first theme in Grades 1–6 suggest ways to gauge your students' strengths and needs during the first few weeks of school. These pages contain information on informal and formal assessment, on diagnosing student needs, and on estimating fluency. They also identify resources in HOUGHTON MIFFLIN READING that will help you to differentiate instruction.

	Instructional Goal	Indicators	Assessment Activity	Assessment Method
Grades K–2	Use Story Structure to summarize a story	■ sequences ideas clearly ■ includes/describes characters ■ identifies story problem	■ The student orally retells a story he or she has read. ■ The student makes a picture map to retell the story.	■ teacher observation notes ■ Retelling Checklist
Grades 3–6	Use Story Structure to summarize a story	■ conveys mood/feeling of original story ■ summarizes actions/events ■ accurately relates main idea/problem ■ uses supporting details ■ accurately describes characters and character traits ■ accurately relates resolution	■ The student writes a story summary. ■ The student makes a story map to summarize the story.	■ Retelling Rubric ■ teacher-student conference ■ Theme Skills Test

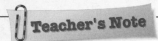

Teacher's Note

Teacher Self-Assessment Does your assessment plan

- match instruction?
- include a variety of authentic tasks?
- include both formal and informal measures?
- extend over time?
- allow for student differences?
- engage students in thinking about and assessing their own learning?

Starting Out

Starting Out margin notes appear throughout this handbook as a guide to the basics of an assessment-based literacy classroom.

Review the Assessment Planning Guide on page 90 for a sample assessment plan.

Keep these suggestions in mind as you develop an assessment-based instructional plan for your classroom.

1. Include both informal and formal assessment measures.

Informal assessment is any assessment procedure that occurs as part of the instructional process. Examples include

- student work samples
- teacher observational notes and inventories
- checklists and forms, such as the Oral Reading Record
- student self-assessment activities

Generally, formal assessment is any measure of student learning that is conducted with a test. Standardized tests, classroom spelling tests, and end-of-unit theme tests are examples of formal assessment. Increasingly, standardized formal assessment instruments include authentic assessment activities—for example, writing activities that allow students to synthesize what they have learned and demonstrate their progress in several areas at once.

Before students are formally assessed on their achievement of a particular goal, make sure that they have had opportunities to learn or practice the skill, concept, or process it involves. Use these instructional activities as a chance to conduct informal assessments of student progress toward the goal.

2. Include authentic tasks.
Assessment is authentic when students demonstrate what they know by doing meaningful tasks. Try to provide multiple opportunities for authentic assessment, using real-world literacy activities such as conducting interviews, writing letters, discussing literature, creating drawings, and making presentations.

3. Include a variety of tasks with the same learning outcome.
Multiple indicators give students a chance to show what they know in different ways. Also, to the extent that the tasks are authentic, they also serve to strengthen students' grasp of a skill or deepen their understanding of a concept. Further, given adequate opportunities, students with varying abilities and language proficiency can demonstrate their learning.

For example, if your instructional goal is to have students show that they recognize how a character feels, you might

- ask a first-grader to draw a picture to show how the character feels;
- ask an older student to role-play a character in a new situation;
- ask others to work with partners as they describe orally what a character was feeling.

The chart on page 7 shows how different tasks can demonstrate evidence of the same skills while providing a balance of formal and informal assessment measures.

4. **Assess throughout the grading period.** Reading, writing, speaking, listening, and viewing are complex processes that develop over time. By including a variety of informal assessment measures over an extended period of time, you give students many opportunities to show what they know. This accommodates different abilities as well as different rates of learning, and it relieves the pressure that can surround formal tests. In addition, it allows you to assess how students have grown over time.

5. **Involve your students in their own assessment.** In an assessment-based literacy classroom, teachers *and* students are the primary evaluators. You may be accustomed to your role as an evaluator, but your students will need your support in thinking about and assessing their own learning. As part of your instructional plan, then, you should make sure that students know not only the goals of instruction but also the criteria by which their work or learning will be judged. Ultimately, students will be able to take a more active role in assessment by helping you develop assessment criteria. In doing so, they will develop a greater sense of ownership of their own learning and a better understanding of the criteria for good work. (For more on student self-assessment, see pages 31–32 of Part 5.)

Teacher's Note

Managing Assessment Materials

- Shared materials—writing and other work samples, drawings, and photographs of projects—can easily be kept in students' portfolios. (For more on portfolios, see pages 22–23 of Part 5.)

- Confidential materials, such as anecdotal records, certain checklists (see Part 10), and test scores, can be stored in an evaluation notebook—a large three-ring binder with a tabbed section for each student. Include some blank paper in each section as well to record notes on various activities or simply to provide a place for observations written on sticky notes or labels.

  If the notebook becomes full, you may want to store the records from previous grading periods in a box or use a separate notebook for each grading period.

- The *Learner Profile*™ CD-ROM available with HOUGHTON MIFFLIN READING, lets you record, manage, and report your assessment of student progress electronically. Companion software *Learner Profile to Go*™ allows you to record student information on a handheld computer device.

Part 4

Beginning the Year: Screening, Diagnosis, and Instructional Planning

Starting Out

You might want to use these questions in your conferences with students.

- Tell me about a book you like.
- How do you feel about reading?
- Who is a good reader that you know?
- What makes a person a good reader?

Program Resources

Back to School launches each level of HOUGHTON MIFFLIN READING at Grades 1–6. The activities shown in the *Teacher's Edition* provide opportunities for initial informal assessment of students' phonemic awareness/phonics skills, reading strategies, and participation in class discussions. Learning More About Your Students and Planning for Instruction pages following the Strategy Workshop give information on assessing instructional strengths and needs.

Introduction

At the beginning of the year, getting to know your students will help you to build a preliminary instructional plan. These ideas might help you learn more about your students.

- Have a conference with each student. In the first two weeks, try to meet with each student for about five minutes. Ask students about their interests and their attitudes toward reading and writing. Prepare a brief list of questions to focus the discussion.

- Review any portfolios from previous years.

- Have students read aloud to check for fluency.

- Ask them to provide a writing sample on a topic of their choice.

- Watch how students work together on a small-group activity.

- Use the checklists and forms in Part 10 to assess students informally. Examples include the Student Interest Inventory on page 91, the Kindergarten Observation Checklists beginning on page 93, and the Reading Attitudes and Habits Inventory on page 109.

- Use the initial assessment tools described here to help determine reading abilities and learning needs.

Initial Screening and Diagnostic Assessment Tools

THE *EMERGING LITERACY SURVEY*

Houghton Mifflin's *Emerging Literacy Survey* can be used to document the emerging literacy skills that children bring with them to kindergarten, to first grade, or to an intervention or remediation program. The survey quickly assesses several areas related to the success of beginning readers (Grades K–2). It is meant to be used flexibly, with other assessment measures.

You can use the *Emerging Literacy Survey* to

- identify children's strengths so you can build instruction upon what they already know;

- select candidates for early intervention;

- establish a baseline from which to chart progress in areas such as phonemic awareness, familiarity with print, beginning reading, and beginning writing.

The survey is designed to be administered to one child at a time, but some sections can be given in small groups. Each section begins with directions and practice items that familiarize the child with the procedure.

Because literacy develops uniquely in each child, any errors made at this level should be viewed as valuable sources of information about growth rather than simply as a score. Assessment at this level focuses on understanding what the child understands about specific concepts of language.

THE *LEXIA QUICK PHONICS ASSESSMENT CD-ROM*

The *Lexia Quick Phonics Assessment CD-ROM* (for Macintosh and Windows) will help you evaluate the phonics and decoding skills of students in Grades K–6.

The CD-ROM's twelve tests include two word tests and two nonword (pseudoword) tests at each of three levels: K–1, 2, and 3–6. A test program works like this:

- A letter, word, or nonword is displayed on the computer screen.

- The student responds verbally; then an adult presses a key to indicate whether the response is right or wrong.

- A new test item appears on the screen.

- When a student being tested at Level K–1 or Level 2 makes two or more mistakes in a skills test, the software branches to a subsection test to assess the skill area in more depth. If the student makes many errors early in the K–1 test, the test ends early to prevent discouragement.

ESPECIALLY FOR KINDERGARTEN

The *Emerging Literacy Survey* can be administered during the first few weeks of school. The other assessments appropriate for Kindergarten may be used several weeks later.

- The software records the student's accuracy and speed of response, scores the test, analyzes the results, and issues a performance report. It identifies the skills mastered, skills needing practice, and skills requiring additional instruction.

- If additional instruction is indicated, the program prescribes units in two pieces of instructional software, the *Lexia Phonics CD-ROM: Primary Intervention* (K–2) and the *Lexia Phonics CD-ROM: Intermediate Intervention* (3–6).

In addition to individual performance reports, the software can generate progress reports after repeat testing and class reports after all students have been tested.

THE *HOUGHTON MIFFLIN PHONICS/ DECODING SCREENING TEST*

The *Houghton Mifflin Phonics/Decoding Screening Test* is useful in determining the ability of a student in Grades 1–6 to use knowledge of sound/letter correspondences (phonics) to decode words. This test will pinpoint areas in which the student needs explicit phonics instruction, and it will also help you select reading tasks that will be most effective in reinforcing the skills the student does possess.

Here are some of the test's features.

- It is individually administered and takes just 15–25 minutes.

- Each task presents letters and words (from simple one-syllable to multisyllabic words) for a student to identify or decode. Pseudowords (made-up words) are included since the student must use decoding skills to correctly pronounce these words and cannot have memorized them.

- The test manual helps you score, summarize, and analyze the results and customize your instruction.

THE *BASELINE GROUP TESTS*

Results obtained with the *Baseline Group Tests,* given at the beginning of the year, serve as general indicators of the amount of reading support individual students will need.

- Each grade level (1–6) has its own test booklet, which begins with a Practice Test to familiarize students with the test format.

- Each test consists of two reading passages, each followed by comprehension questions. At Grades 1–2 both passages are fiction. At Grades 3–6 the first passage is fiction and the second is nonfiction.

- The questions for Grade 1 are in a multiple-choice format; at Grades 2–6, questions are in both written-response and multiple-choice formats.

- The Teacher's Annotated Edition for each grade level explains how to score the test, explains how to estimate an appropriate reading level, and helps you identify the amount of instructional support needed.

Students may be able to complete the two passages and their accompanying questions in one class period. However, you may need or prefer to use two class periods to administer the test.

THE *LEVELED READING PASSAGES ASSESSMENT KIT*

The *Leveled Reading Passages Assessment Kit* provides you with the materials you need to assess and evaluate students' reading levels at Grades K–6. The kit contains twenty-two small Leveled Reading Books (two at each of eleven reading levels), as well as a set of blackline masters (word lists, scoring sheets, and summaries).

The Leveled Reading Books present a variety of types of text, and they appeal to a wide range of interests. Their content is developmentally appropriate for the reading level. Many leveling criteria, including the following, have also been taken into account:

- sentence length and complexity
- paragraph length
- vocabulary and high-frequency-word recognition
- decodability
- type size and style
- picture-text ratio

Program Resources

Meeting Individual Needs

- The *Extra Support Handbook* has lessons and selection previews to help you meet learning needs.

- The *Handbook for English Language Learners* helps you meet the needs of students whose primary language is not English.

- The *Challenge Handbook* has projects and activities for your most advanced students.

- The *Classroom Management Handbook* helps you organize time and materials to facilitate work with groups; it includes independent activities.

Using Assessment to Meet Individual Needs

Using appropriate assessment measures can help you identify a student's individual learning needs. Throughout the year, you may want to use the individual Informal Assessment Checklists on pages 99 and 100 of this handbook to appraise each student's strengths and needs.

As you consider how to assess learning in your classroom, include appropriate procedures for English language learners and for learners with special needs. For more discussion about assessment to meet individual needs, see Part 9, which begins on page 78.

Planning Instruction

The chart below outlines the skills and abilities you might want to assess at the beginning of the year and shows the tools that can help you. It also shows program resources in HOUGHTON MIFFLIN READING that you can use in planning instruction.

TE: Teacher's Edition   **TRB:** Teacher's Resource Blackline Masters   **PB:** Practice Book   **BLMs:** Blackline Masters   **Parenthetical numbers:** grade levels

If you want to assess...	You can use...	Then you can...	
		give extra support	**challenge**
Concepts of Print	Emerging Literacy Survey	TE: special attention to Concepts of Print boxes **(K–1)**	Little Big Books **(K–1)** Theme Paperbacks (above level) **(1)**
Letter Naming	Emerging Literacy Survey	TE: Reteaching lessons for Phonics **(1)** *Extra Support Handbook* **(K)**	Move more quickly from letter-naming into phonics **(K)**
Word Recognition	Emerging Literacy Survey	TE, Resources: Reteaching lessons for Phonics, High-Frequency Words **(1)**	Theme Paperbacks (above level), Little Big Books **(1)**

If you want to assess...	You can use...	Then you can...	
		give extra support	challenge
Word Writing	Emerging Literacy Survey	TE: special emphasis on High-Frequency Words lessons; Building Words **(K)**; Spelling **(1)**	Writing Center activities: writing sentences; journal writing **(K–1)**
Phonemic Awareness and Phonics/Decoding	TE: Back to School: Letter Recognition, Phonemic Awareness, Phonics Review Lessons **(1)**; Phonics Review Lessons **(2)** Emerging Literacy Survey Phonics/Decoding Screening Test **(1–6)** Leveled Reading Passages **(K–6)** Lexia Quick Phonics Assessment CD-ROM **(K–6)**	TE: Phonemic Awareness activities in Opening Routines and Phonics sections **(K–1)**; Extra Support/Intervention boxes, Monitoring Student Progress in Phonics lessons **(K–2)**; Phonics Center activities **(K–1)**; Listening Center: Alphafriend Audios, Alphafolders **(K)** TE, Resources: Reteaching Lessons for Phonics **(1–2)** Other Reading: Phonics Library BLMs; On My Way Practice Readers **(K)** CD-ROMs: *Lexia Phonics Primary Intervention* **(K–2)**, *Intermediate Intervention* **(3–6)**; *Get Set for Reading* **(1–6)**; *Curious George Learns Phonics* **(K–2)**	Other Reading: Little Big Books **(K–1)**, Classroom Bookshelf **(K–6)**
Structural Analysis/ Phonics	TE: Back to School: Phonics/ Decoding Lesson **(3–6)** Phonics/Decoding Screening Test **(1–6)** Lexia Quick Phonics Assessment CD-ROM **(K–6)**	TE, Resources: Reteaching Lessons for Structural Analysis Skills **(3–6)** Other Reading: Leveled Readers BLMs **(3–6)**; Theme Paperbacks (below level), Classroom Bookshelf (below level) **(K–6)** *Extra Support Handbook* **(3–6)** CD-ROMs: *Get Set for Reading* **(1–6)**; *Lexia Phonics Intermediate Intervention* **(3–6)**	TE, Resources: Challenge/ Extension Activities for Phonics **(1–2)** Other Reading: Theme Paperbacks (above level), Classroom Bookshelf **(K–6)** CD-ROM: *Wacky Web Tales* **(3–6)**

If you want to assess...	You can use...	Then you can...	
		give extra support	**challenge**
High-Frequency Words	Leveled Reading Passages **(K–6)**	TE: Monitoring Student Progress, High-Frequency Word Practice in Word Work sections **(K)** TE, Resources: Reteaching Lessons for High-Frequency Words **(1–2)** Other Reading: On My Way Practice Readers **(K)**; Phonics Library BLMs **(K–2)** *Extra Support Handbook* **(K–2)**	TE, Resources: Challenge/ Extension Activities for High-Frequency Words **(1–2)** Other Reading: Little Big Books **(K–2)**, Classroom Bookshelf **(K–6)**
Reading Strategies	TE: Back to School: Strategy Workshop **(1–6)** Leveled Reading Passages **(K–6)**	TE, each selection: Extra Support/Intervention boxes **(1–6)** TE: Strategy **(K)**; Strategy Focus, Extra Support/ Intervention Strategy modeling **(1–6)**; Strategy Review **(3–6)** Big Books **(1–2)** PB: Strategy Poster **(1–6)** *Extra Support Handbook* (Phonics Decoding Strategy) **(K–6)**	TE, each selection: Challenge boxes **(1)** Other Reading: Theme Paperbacks (above level) **(1–6)**; Classroom Bookshelf **(1–6)**
Comprehension/ Comparing Texts	Baseline Group Test **(1–6)** Leveled Reading Passages **(K–6)**	TE: Retelling or Summarizing prompts in Responding section **(K)**; Building Background **(K–6)**; Key Concepts **(K–3)** TE, each selection: Extra Support/Intervention boxes, Writing Support for Responding, Previewing the Selection boxes **(1–6)**	TE: Center Activities in Responding section **(K)** TE, each selection: Challenge boxes **(K–6)** and Assignment Cards **(2–6)**; Responding questions and activities **(K–2)** TE, Resources: Challenge/ Extension Activities for Comprehension **(1–6)**

If you want to assess...	You can use...	Then you can...	
		give extra support	**challenge**
Comprehension/ Comparing Texts (continued)		Comprehension Review Lessons **(2–6)** TE, Resources: Reteaching Lessons for Comprehension Skills **(1–6)** TRB: Selection Summaries **(1–6)** Other Reading: On My Way Practice Readers, Phonics Library BLMs **(K–2)**; Leveled Readers BLMs **(3–6)**; Theme Paperbacks (below level) **(1–6)**, Classroom Bookshelf (below level) **(K–6)** CD-ROM: *Get Set for Reading* **(1–6)** Anthology Audios **(1–6)** *Extra Support Handbook* **(1–6)**	Other Reading: Little Big Books **(K–2)**, Classroom Bookshelf **(K–6)**, Theme Paperbacks (above level books) **(1–6)**, Classroom Bookshelf (above level) **(K–6)** *Challenge Handbook* **(K–6)**
Spelling	Phonics/Decoding Screening Test **(1–6)**	TE, each selection: Basic Words, Extra Support/Intervention box in Spelling lesson **(1–6)**	TE, each selection: Challenge Words, Challenge box in Spelling lesson **(1–6)**
Writing	Baseline Group Test **(1–6)**	TE: Shared, Interactive Independent Writing **(K)** TE, Reading-Writing Workshop: Student Writing Model, Writing Traits notes, Student Self-Assessment **(1–6)**	TE, each selection: Journal Writing, Genre Lessons, Writer's Craft Lessons **(1–6)** TE, Reading-Writing Workshop: Reading as a Writer, Publishing and Evaluating **(1–6)** TE, Resources: Writing Activities **(2–6)** *Challenge Handbook* **(K–6)**
English Language Proficiency	Checklists in Part 10 and in *Handbook for English Language Learners*	*Handbook for English Language Learners*	*Handbook for English Language Learners*

Ongoing Informal Assessment

Introduction

Ongoing informal assessment, as its name implies, involves your daily observation and analysis of both how students learn and work and what they create to express themselves and demonstrate learning. Any of the following may be elements in ongoing informal assessment:

- journal entries, writing folders, learning logs, workbooks
- participation in discussions
- oral presentations
- running records, retellings, and summaries
- student interest surveys
- conferences, interviews, conversations
- anecdotal notes, checklists, and forms

The teacher constantly assesses process and product—and that assessment informs subsequent instructional activities. Ideally, ongoing informal assessment and instruction merge seamlessly.

Ongoing informal assessment also involves student self-assessment. Using a variety of devices, students can learn to assess their own learning and contribute insights that may help shape your instructional plans.

Some of the benefits of ongoing informal assessment are these.

- It lets you determine the pace and the nature of instruction.
- It enables you to focus on what happens in the classroom, what students are able to do, and how they go about doing it.
- When used together with formal assessment measures as part of a balanced assessment program, it provides information that can guide instruction and give you a broader and more detailed view of the whole student.

Observing Students

Observing students engaged in the *process* of an activity, both when you are directly involved with them and when you are not directly involved, will help you understand how they understand and how they create or arrive at the *product*.

You can observe students as you talk with them during interviews or conferences, for example, and as you conduct fluency checks or listen to retellings or summaries. You can also observe students as they work independently in cooperative group activities, dramatic play, oral discussions, journal writing, and Reading-Writing Workshops.

You can easily record your observations on observation checklists or as anecdotal records. Checklists and notes from observations are useful for

- tracking learning in progress;
- planning instruction;
- writing comments on report cards;
- understanding student attitudes, habits, and learning strategies;
- understanding the process involved in creating a product;
- supporting evaluations shared with parents, administrators, and students during conferences.

As you observe your students over time, you will gain an expanded view of their literacy development. Refer to the Assessment Planning Guide on page 90 of this handbook for suggestions on scheduling observations. Your decision on when to record your observations, however, will depend on your needs and time constraints.

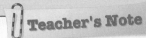

Teacher's Note

Managing Ongoing Informal Assessment

- Set goals for what you are going to assess. For example, you might focus on listening and speaking skills by observing each student in a group discussion.

- Plan how often you write notes on each student for those skills. For example, one week you might take notes on three students each day. This will ensure that you cover all students every two weeks.

- Go slowly, adding one new assessment method at a time.

- Let student needs guide your decisions. Not all assessment activities need to be done for all students at all times.

- Decide how you will make notes and record observations. Some teachers record notes directly in a notebook. Others use a clipboard to hold sticky notes, labels, index cards, or checklists until they can transfer the notes to individual student records in an evaluation notebook (see box on page 9 in Part 3).

- Record observations while they are still fresh in your mind.

The *Teacher's Resource Blackline Masters* includes an Observation Checklist for each week (Grade 1) or each theme (Grades 2–6) that focuses on the goals for the week/theme. An Observation Checklist for each theme also appears in the *Teacher's Edition* for Kindergarten. Each of the Kindergarten Observation Checklists on pages 93–98 of this handbook covers a skill area, such as phonemic awareness, and can be used across themes or for observing several students.

· Houghton Mifflin ·
Reading

Starting Out

Start Small Begin by focusing on one area, such as reading. Decide which reading goals you will assess and how often you will assess them. Set an achievable goal. For example, choose one or two checklists to fill out for each student once a month.

OBSERVATION CHECKLISTS

You may find it convenient to record observations on checklists. Part 10 of this handbook contains a number of Observation Checklists, most of which can be used to observe individuals or groups. Several are designed specifically for use with early readers (Grades K–1). Use an Observation Checklist

- as you review a student's writing and spelling skills;
- to note a student's reading, writing, and work habits;
- to note speaking, listening, and viewing behaviors;
- to note a student's ability for self-assessment;
- before introducing a theme or selection, to plan your goals and instruction;
- for identifying and diagnosing instructional needs.

ANECDOTAL RECORDS

Anecdotal records are brief notes about a specific student in a specific learning situation. They are useful for

- guiding conferences with students and parents,
- setting instructional goals,
- writing narratives on report cards,
- recording information about both process and product.

Your anecdotal records will be most helpful to you if you

- take notes in a variety of settings,
- describe a single observation,
- relate your observation to known facts about the student,
- focus on what the student is doing.

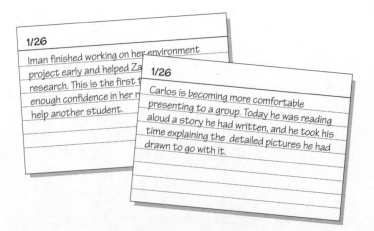

1/26

Iman finished working on her environment project early and helped Za... research. This is the first t... enough confidence in her r... help another student.

1/26

Carlos is becoming more comfortable presenting to a group. Today he was reading aloud a story he had written, and he took his time explaining the detailed pictures he had drawn to go with it.

Assessing Student Work

WORK SAMPLES

Besides your observations, a major resource for ongoing informal assessment is the oral, written, and graphic work that students produce in the course of their instructional activities. These products are, for the most part, tangible evidence of what students are learning, and, as such, can help you continuously shape instruction to meet student needs.

Here is an example from first grade. Simon has completed the *Practice Book* phonics activity pages on words with the long-*i* sound (pages 33 and 34). For the most part, he did well writing the long-*i* words on page 33, where the letters are provided for him. His performance on page 34, however, tells you that he hears all the sounds in the long-*i* words and spells them sequentially but has trouble remembering to add the final *e*. Based on your assessment of these pages, you might put Simon in a small group and use the Reteaching lesson on page R12 of the Grade 1 *Teacher's Edition*. Then, to assess his improvement, you might ask Simon to read to you the first page of the Phonics Library book *Pine Lake*. As he reads, you note whether he uses the short-*i* sound in *Rick* and the long-*i* sound in all the words with the CVC-*e* pattern.

In this Grade 4 example, Alina has completed the *Practice Book* pages on the comprehension skill Topic, Main Idea, and Supporting Details (pages 208 and 211). Your review of page 208 tells you that Alina had trouble identifying main ideas as she read *Wildfires* in her Anthology. Her work on page 211, which she completed after your Comprehension Skills lesson, shows improvement but indicates that she still might benefit from the Reteaching lesson on the skill.

Similarly, as you read student writing, you can assess how well students have understood an assignment, how well they organize and present information and ideas, and how advanced their word choice, sentence fluency, and command of language conventions are. Reviewing graphic organizers and successive drafts of students' Reading-Writing Workshop pieces will tell you even more, including how well students use the writing process. (For more on evaluating student writing, see Part 6, on page 36.)

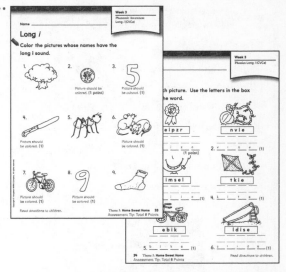

Grade 1 Practice Book, *pages 33 and 34*

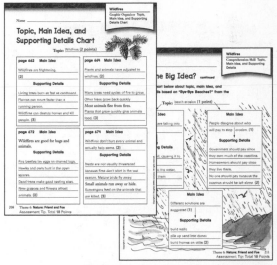

Grade 4 Practice Book, *pages 208 and 211*

Program Resources

Monitoring Student Progress in the skills lessons provided in the *Teacher's Edition* guide you in planning instruction based on students' work in the *Practice Book*. See page 23 in this handbook for more information.

Portfolio Opportunity reminders in the *Teacher's Edition* and *Practice Book* of HOUGHTON MIFFLIN READING help you collect a broad sample of student work.

See also Using Multiple Measures in each Theme Wrap-Up.

· Houghton Mifflin ·
Reading

ESPECIALLY FOR GRADES K–2

Younger students should be allowed to help select portfolio samples. Even the youngest child, when reviewing journal entries collected over time, can identify areas of growth and strength. You can record each student's comments and evaluation of his or her work during individual interviews.

ESPECIALLY FOR GRADES 3–6

Gradually turning over to students the job of organizing and updating the portfolio encourages them to develop their organizational and self-assessment strategies. Set aside time on a regular basis, perhaps once or twice a month, for students to review and reorganize their work and to think about their progress.

PORTFOLIOS

Portfolios—selective collections of student work compiled over time—are an invaluable aid in your assessment of student products and, to some degree, their processes as well. Besides providing a balanced array of information to help you measure student progress and identify instructional needs, portfolios also serve to encourage student goal-setting and self-assessment. Further, they allow you to show parents a comprehensive picture of their children's performance.

Selecting Materials for the Portfolio

Both you and your students should have a role in selecting pieces for the portfolio. Work to be included might be selected because it is

- generally noteworthy,
- an example of a particular skill,
- an example of a particular kind of writing,
- a good example of a particular criterion,
- an example from a certain time in the school year,
- a typical example of the student's work.

For several pieces of work selected, have students complete a cover sheet giving title, date of completion, and a reason for inclusion in the portfolio.

Reviewing Portfolios

Part of portfolio assessment includes regular reviews of the portfolio contents. Try to plan portfolio reviews at least once or twice a month. Make note of

- indicators in students' work of a need for extra support or challenge;
- students' progress in meeting their own goals and assessing their own work.

During portfolio reviews, you may want to reread any observation records, conference notes, and anecdotal records that are *not* kept in portfolios to help you further assess students' learning needs.

Portfolio Conferences

The variety of samples included and the students' role in selecting and evaluating their work make portfolios ideal for use in conferences.

- Brief **Teacher-Student Conferences**, conducted with one or two students or one small group per day, give you time to discuss progress, strategies, goals, and selection of work samples with students. This time also allows you to observe and informally assess each student closely and to model and encourage student self-assessment and goal-setting. You might want to record notes—with the student looking on—about the strengths of the student's work, areas needing improvement, how the student can improve in these areas, and the student's goals for the next time period or project. Keep these notes in your evaluation notebook.

- **Peer Conferences** give students a chance to share pieces they choose from their portfolios with each other and receive feedback in specific areas. Be sure to model good conference behavior that focuses on the positive aspects of students' work.

- **Teacher-Parent Conferences** can help parents gain a better understanding of their child's strengths and needs. You may want to invite students to participate during part of these parent conferences.

Home/Community Connection

Teacher-Parent Conferences

Before you meet with a student's parent(s), choose a few samples of tests, surveys, or inventories and work from the student's portfolio. Be prepared to comment on each sample.

Some other topics to discuss:

- Student's areas of strength
- Areas needing improvement
- What is being done in class to foster improvement
- What parents can do to help
- Overall progress being made
- Goals the student has set

Assessing Reading

MONITORING STUDENT PROGRESS BOXES

A Back to School selection introduces each grade level of HOUGHTON MIFFLIN READING. As you work through this selection, refer to the Monitoring Student Progress boxes for help with evaluating your students' use of reading strategies.

Numerous Monitoring Student Progress checks are also provided in the *Teacher's Edition.* These appear

- at the end of each literature selection segment, to check reading strategies;

- in the Phonics (K, Day 4; Grades 1–2), Structural Analysis (Grades 3–6), Comprehension Skills, High-Frequency Words (Grades K–2), Vocabulary Skills and Grammar Skills (Grades 2–6) lessons that support each selection;

Monitoring Student Progress	
If . . .	**Then . . .**
students have difficulty summarizing the story,	use a Graphic Organizer to chart where the story takes place, who the main characters are, what the problem is, and what happens in the beginning, middle, and end. Then have students use the information on the chart to summarize the story.

- in each skill Reteaching lesson (Resources, Grades 1–6).

The "If . . . /You can . . ." structure and specific suggestions of the Monitoring Student Progress checks are designed to help you plan instruction.

COMPREHENSION CHECKS

In the *Teacher's Edition*, a Comprehension Check accompanies the Responding pages following each selection. It directs you to a *Practice Book* page that assesses students' understanding of the selection. This feature helps you easily determine whether extra support on comprehension is needed for some students.

SELECTION TESTS

Each two-page Selection Test in the *Teacher's Resource Blackline Masters* consists of both open-response and multiple-choice questions intended to assess the students' selection comprehension and vocabulary. One question focuses on the lesson's reading strategy, which students must apply in order to answer correctly. As they proceed through a test, students are allowed to review the selection. An Answer Key follows the tests.

RETELLINGS AND SUMMARIES

Retelling is a strategy for assessing comprehension by asking a student to retell orally or in writing what was read. You can begin simply by saying, "Now, start at the beginning, and you tell me that story. Tell it in your own words." The setting for retellings should be relaxed and informal.

Retellings can also be written, using a number of forms:

- picture mapping (retelling the story in pictures)
- Venn diagrams (retelling two stories by comparing and contrasting)
- story mapping (retelling the structure and elements of a story by noting character, setting, problem, events, and resolution)
- story frames (writing main ideas in frames)
- time line (for nonfiction)

Another, more difficult, form of retelling is the oral or written summary. You can ask students to summarize a story, highlighting only the main idea and important events.

The following rubric can be used to score a student's retelling.

Retelling Scoring Rubric			
4	**3**	**2**	**1**
Includes the main idea or problem, all significant events or information, many supporting details; retelling is organized in proper sequence and is coherent.	Includes the main idea or problem, most significant events, some details; may miss the resolution; may include some minor misinformation; retelling is generally organized and sequenced.	Has some information from the passage but misses the main idea or problem; may have a few key events, information, or details but not integrated into the larger story; little organization or sequence	Little or no content is included in the retelling; may include some points from the passage, mostly details, but misses the main idea or problem and significant ideas; retelling is unfocused, sketchy; misinformation or little information

FLUENCY

Fluency is a general term that comprises reading rate (words per minute), reading accuracy, and phrasing, flow, and expressiveness.

Fluency assessments can provide a wealth of information about your students' reading abilities. They can help you

- evaluate students' reading behaviors;
- plan instruction;
- check the appropriateness of the text for the student;
- monitor progress.

When measuring fluency, it is important to use an on-level text. However, be aware that a child's overall fluency can vary according to a text's relative difficulty, its topic, and its genre. Also, fluency can be affected by a child's familiarity—or inexperience—with the text to be read.

Because conducting a fluency assessment involves certain recording conventions, you may want to have a teacher trained in the process demonstrate it for you. Basically, for one minute you will observe and record everything a student says and does while reading aloud from a sample text (about 100 to 150 words).

If possible, have a copy of the text that you can mark, or use the Oral Reading Record on page 102 of this handbook. Follow these directions if you use the Oral Reading Record.

- For each line of the passage, write a check for each word read correctly.

Program Resources

- An Anthology selection that can be used to practice or assess fluency is suggested in the Fluency Practice note with each main literature selection in HOUGHTON MIFFLIN READING.

- Alternatively, you can use a passage from the appropriate level of the *Leveled Reading Passages Assessment Kit*. The kit includes twenty-two leveled passages, blackline master score sheets for each passage, and detailed instructions for using both to take oral reading records.

Oral Reading Record

Student's Name Billy M.

Book In the Woods   Date Dec. 2

L1 ✓✓✓✓✓✓✓✓
L2 ✓✓✓✓✓✓✓
L3 ✓✓
L4 ✓✓✓✓✓✓✓
L5 ✓✓✓✓✓✓ (cracked) ✓
L6 ✓✓✓ (children) ✓✓✓
L7 ✓✓✓✓✓✓✓✓
L8 ✓✓✓✓ splash SC
L9 (splish) splash ✓✓✓✓✓
L10 ✓✓✓✓✓✓
L11 (catching) ✓✓✓
L12 ✓✓✓✓✓
L13 ✓✓✓✓✓
L14
L15

Reading rate (WCPM): 78 Progress: ☐ Expected ☑ Below expected ☐ Seriously below expected

Decoding accuracy: Number of words read correctly ÷ Number of words in passage = ___ / ___ = ___ %

Phrasing and expression (see Teacher's Assessment Handbook, page 26): ___ score

Comments: stops at longer words—needs to look at middles and ends of words

Teacher's Assessment Handbook ①

Teacher's Note

Self-Timed Fluency Check

Occasionally, you may want to have your students do self-assessments for fluency, using easy text or text they have been tested on before. Many students enjoy timing themselves and are encouraged when they have clear evidence of their reading progress. Make sure that you check to see that students don't emphasize rate over accuracy and comprehension.

- Write on the appropriate line, and count as an error, each mispronunciation or substitution. Write the word from the text on the line and the word the child says above the line.

- Write on the line, circle, and count as an error each omission or word not read or self-corrected within three seconds (after three seconds, tell the student the word).

- Do not count self-corrections as errors. Write the word from the text on the line, the word the child says above the line, and the letters *SC* to indicate immediate self-correction.

- Mark the last word read at the end of a minute, but allow the student to continue reading to the end of the sentence.

- Calculate the score as follows:
  Words Per Minute ____
  Minus Incorrect Words ____
  Words Correct Per Minute (WCPM) ____

Use the chart on page 27 to translate student scores into degrees of progress. Record the student's reading rate, degree of progress, and decoding accuracy score on the Oral Reading Record. Then record a score for phrasing and expression as determined by the scoring rubric below.

Beginning readers and older readers who have difficulty with fluency will benefit from further instruction and from fluency testing every four to six weeks. Stronger readers can be assessed every two to three months.

Scoring Rubric for Phrasing and Expression			
4	**3**	**2**	**1**
Reads primarily in larger, meaningful phrases. Although the student may make some errors or repetitions, these do not appear to detract from the overall structure of the story. Most of the story is read with expressive interpretation, guided by meaning and punctuation.	Reads primarily in three- or four-word phrases, although there are some word-by-word slowdowns. However, the majority of phrasing seems appropriate and preserves the author's meaning. Some expressive interpretation is evident.	Reads primarily in two-word phrases with some three- and four-word groupings. Some word-by-word reading may be present. Word groupings may seem awkward and unrelated to meaning. Little expressive interpretation is evident.	Reads primarily word by word. Two- or three-word phrases may occur occasionally, but these are infrequent and/or they do not preserve meaning. No expression is evident.

	Scores = Words Correct Per Minute (WCPM)		
Grade 1			**Late Grade 1**
Expected Progress			40–60
Below Expected Progress			0–39
Grade 2	**Early Grade 2**	**Mid-Grade 2**	**Late Grade 2**
Expected Progress	53–82	78–106	94–124
Below Expected Progress	23–52	46–77	65–93
Seriously Below Expected Progress	0–22	0–45	0–64
Grade 3	**Early Grade 3**	**Mid-Grade 3**	**Late Grade 3**
Expected Progress	79–110	93–123	114–142
Below Expected Progress	65–78	70–92	87–113
Seriously Below Expected Progress	0–64	0–69	0–86
Grade 4	**Early Grade 4**	**Mid-Grade 4**	**Late Grade 4**
Expected Progress	99–125	112–133	118–145
Below Expected Progress	72–98	89–111	92–117
Seriously Below Expected Progress	0–71	0–88	0–91
Grades 5–6	**Early Grades 5–6**	**Mid-Grades 5–6**	**Late Grades 5–6**
Expected Progress	106–132	118–143	128–151
Below Expected Progress	77–105	93–117	100–127
Seriously Below Expected Progress	0–76	0–92	0–99

Table uses data adapted from Hasbrouck, Jan E. and Tindal, Gerald. "Curriculum-Based Oral Reading Fluency Norms for Students in Grades 2 Through 5." *Teaching Exceptional Children*. Spring, 1992, p. 41.

Timed Fluency Tests

To gauge the effectiveness of your instruction with struggling first-grade readers, you might want to measure their progress in reading lists of words. At the end of each theme, you can test the children you're most concerned about to determine how steady their improvement is and whether reteaching is required.

Use the Word-Reading Fluency blackline master on page 103 of this handbook. It is a randomized collection of decodable words taught in the entire Grade 1 year. At the end of each theme, test the children you're concerned about. Realize that at the beginning, children will know few of the words. Over time, however, you should see steady progress in the number of words children can read successfully. You can time children to check for automaticity in their word-reading as well. If a child is unable to read a word after three seconds, direct him or her to the next word. Again, you'll be tracking children's progress across themes.

Program Resources

If you want to check certain children's word reading after each selection, use the Alternative Assessment provided for each week in the Teacher's Resource Blackline Masters. It contains a list of the high frequency-words of the week and a list of decodable words containing the week's phonic elements.

Houghton Mifflin
Reading

- Make a copy of the blackline master on page 103 for the child to read from and a copy for yourself. Note: Make a version of the blackline master for each theme. Use the same words, but scramble them differently on each version.

- Record words correctly read or, if you time the test, words correct per minute (WCPM) as described on pages 25–26.

- Mark on your copy the letter-sound relationships that the child struggles with; note also whether the child can read words with those same elements after reteaching and whether he or she continues to be successful with those letter-sound associations at the end of the next theme.

- Record children's scores to track progress over time.

If some children make little or no progress across several themes, you might want to instruct them one-on-one for a period and then retest, refer them to your school's reading specialist for more detailed assessment, or begin intervention.

For kindergarten children you're concerned about, you might want to test their letter-naming fluency. Use the Letter-Naming Fluency blackline master on page 104, which contains a mix of upper- and lower-case letters arranged in the order they are taught in HOUGHTON MIFFLIN READING. Again, you can measure children's progress over time, and you might time the test to measure increasing automaticity.

Even if some of your kindergartners continue having trouble naming all the letters for some time, be sure to involve them in your instructional activities for phonemic awareness and phonics. Often letter-naming will develop concurrently with these other literacy skills.

RESPONSE TO LITERATURE

An important aspect of reading assessment is assessing students' response to literature. This response can take many forms, including

- a personal response (an expression of personal feelings inspired by the selection);

- opinions about or interpretations of a selection, supported by references to specific examples from the text;

- indications of literary understanding (comments about the author's craft, literary devices used, text structure);

- comparison of texts;

- references relating a text to prior knowledge or personal experiences.

ESPECIALLY FOR KINDERGARTEN

- You can foster a sense of story sequence and story elements by having children act out or retell stories. Many of the Dramatic Play Center activities offer ideas for retelling or elaborating on a text.

- You can model a personal response to stories you read aloud. You can also relate stories to familiar stories or to your own experience. See the Revisiting the Literature page on Day 5 of every week.

Numerous opportunities for students to respond to literature, both orally and in writing, are provided in HOUGHTON MIFFLIN READING in various forms: comprehension questions, responding activities, journal writing activities, and Literature Discussions. In addition, Writer's Craft and Genre lessons, as well as Focus On Genre in many themes, foster understanding of the elements of literature and enrich student responses. In each theme (Grades 2–6), Check Your Progress asks students to compare fiction and nonfiction selections and to make connections to other theme reading and to their own experience. (See Monitoring Student Progress in your Teacher's Edition.)

There are a number of ways to assess students' response to literature.

- Take anecdotal notes as you observe and listen to students during class discussions, literature circles, retellings, summaries, and dramatic play; you can also use the Response to Literature Checklist on page 107 of this handbook. For Grades K–1 use the Emerging Reading checklist on page 95.

- Read and assess students' written responses to literature.

- Schedule one-on-one conferences every two or three weeks. Ask about the student's current independent-reading book; discuss his or her written responses to literature.

Using a variety of approaches will yield a more complete picture of students' strengths and needs.

Assessing Writing

In most classrooms opportunities for assessing writing abound: you read and review your students' writing, listen to them read their writing, and talk with them about their writing. In HOUGHTON MIFFLIN READING, writing activities may be found in each selection's Writing Skills lesson and Responding pages and each theme's Reading-Writing Workshop and cross-curricular activities.

When assessing writing, ask these questions:

- How comfortable is the student with particular writing formats? writing types?

- Is the student progressing in using the writing process?

- Do the student's confidence and fluency vary in formal and informal writing situations?

- Is the student progressing in specific writing skills, such as organization; use of details; voice and tone; and spelling, grammar, usage, and mechanics?

ESPECIALLY FOR GRADES K–1

When you observe early and emerging writers, the most important thing to look for is that children are learning to use print to convey meaning.

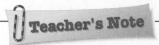

Teacher's Note

When assessing writing, remember that positive reinforcement builds confidence and encourages young writers to take the risks necessary to become better writers. Ultimately, you can help your students to understand and enjoy writing as a way to express ideas.

To track students' progress with the writing process, you may want to use the Writing Process Checklist on page 114 of this handbook. You can find more information on assessing writing in Part 6 of this handbook.

Assessing Listening, Speaking, and Viewing

Students' listening, speaking, and viewing skills can be assessed using informal assessment tools such as anecdotal records and the Listening, Speaking, and Viewing Checklist on page 108. It is important to observe students' behaviors in these skills in a variety of contexts, such as while students

- work in cooperative groups;
- engage in dramatic play and storytelling;
- interact socially with peers;
- retell stories to the class or the teacher;
- view images during classroom activities;
- participate in group discussions;
- present projects to the class or view others' presentations;
- share writing with the class or in small groups;
- follow directions.

As you observe students in various listening, speaking, and viewing activities, look for the development of such behaviors as

- speaking clearly,
- responding to comments or questions,
- listening without interrupting,
- viewing critically to discern important details.

Assessing Attitudes and Habits

Student attitudes and habits about learning and content can be assessed using attitude surveys, inventories, and interviews. Attitudes and habits might be evaluated

- before and after a theme or a project;
- at the beginning and end of the year, or quarterly;
- before introducing a new subject, concept, or skill.

You may wish to use these inventories, found in Part 10 of this handbook: Reading Attitudes and Habits Inventory (page 109), Attitudes and Habits Inventory (Early Writer) (page 110), and Attitudes and Habits Inventory (Fluent Writer) (page 111).

Teacher's Note

Trying to complete surveys and inventories all at the same time can become overwhelming. Instead, use these assessment devices only when you are looking for particular attitudes or habits.

Student Self-Assessment

Involving students in the assessment process is an essential part of an assessment-based literacy classroom. With practice, students who self-assess become more conscious learners, able to apply knowledge of their learning needs and styles to new areas. Further, goal-setting is a natural outgrowth of self-assessment; students who self-assess almost automatically begin to set goals as they see where their work can be improved.

There are two types of self-assessment that students engage in.

- They **reflect** on their reading and their writing, identifying and expressing their feelings: *I liked this story because it's about favorite places, and I have a favorite place.*

- They **evaluate** their work and their learning, analyzing strengths and weaknesses: *I used exact adjectives in my description; I skip hard words when I read.* This kind of self-assessment is more difficult because students do not always know which aspects of their performance they should evaluate or what criteria they should use to evaluate each aspect.

It is important to let students know more specific criteria they should use in thinking about their work. When students understand the criteria for good work before they begin a literacy activity, they are more likely to meet those criteria. As time goes on, you may want to help students set up their own clear criteria for good work.

Self-assessment can take place in many contexts, including the following:

- teacher-student conferences
- discussion (whole class or small groups)
- writing conferences
- reflection logs
- portfolio selection periods
- weekly self-evaluations
- self-assessment checklists and inventories
- teacher-student-parent conferences

You can promote student self-assessment by providing time for students to think, talk, and write about their progress and by modeling reflective and evaluative processes. At first, you can guide student self-assessment with general questions such as these:

Starting Out

Self-Assessment It takes time for students to become comfortable with self-assessment. Start by focusing on one area, such as revising their writing. Gradually work up to having students evaluate their own work in a variety of areas.

Program Resources

The *Teacher's Edition* provides reflective and evaluative self-assessment questions for you to suggest to students

- at the end of each reading selection;
- after each theme's Reading-Writing Workshop.

The *Practice Book* includes a revising checklist for each Reading-Writing Workshop. Students use the checklists to evaluate their drafts before revising.

ESPECIALLY FOR GRADES K–2

Younger children can learn to assess their work, but they may need extra support at first to talk about their ideas. Begin with short class discussions or individual interviews, asking direct, open-ended reflective questions about a specific piece of writing or a drawing. Record the students' responses. Over time move on to evaluative questions that talk about specific criteria.

Evaluative	Reflective
■ What did I do when I came to a word I didn't know?	■ What did I like best about this story I read (piece of writing I did/assignment or activity) and why?
■ What was the hardest part of this paper to write? the easiest?	■ What made me decide to read (write) this piece?
■ What do I need help with to do my best on this assignment?	■ What did I like best about my literature discussion circle today?
■ Is this a good persuasive piece?	
■ Does my story make sense?	
■ Is this book too easy, too hard, or just right for me? Why?	

You may also want to have students complete the Self-Reflection/Self-Assessment sheet on page 92 of this handbook.

Modifying Instruction Based on Ongoing Informal Assessment

The following chart outlines and organizes by skill the ongoing informal assessment tools discussed here. It also lists the resources in HOUGHTON MIFFLIN READING that you can use to provide extra support for and to challenge students.

Note: Remember that you can use students' oral, written, and graphic work for ongoing assessment as well as the instruments listed on the chart.

TE: Teacher's Edition **TRB:** Teacher's Resource Blackline Masters **PB:** Practice Book **BLMs:** Blackline Masters **Parenthetical numbers:** grade levels

If you want to assess...	You can use...	Then you can...	
		give extra support	challenge
Phonemic Awareness and Phonics/Decoding	TE: Monitoring Student Progress **(K–6)** Emerging Literacy Survey Phonics/Decoding Screening Test **(1–6)** Leveled Reading Passages **(K–6)**	TE: Phonemic Awareness activities in Opening Routines and in the Phonics section **(K–1)**; Extra Support/Intervention boxes, Monitoring Student Progress in Phonics lessons **(K–2)**; Phonics Center activities **(K–1)**; Listening Center: Alphafriend Audios, Alphafolders **(K)**	Other Reading: Little Big Books **(K–2)**, Classroom Bookshelf **(K–6)**

If you want to assess...	You can use...	Then you can...	
		give extra support	**challenge**
Phonemic Awareness and Phonics/Decoding (continued)		TE, Resources: Reteaching Lessons for Phonics **(1–2)** Other Reading: Phonics Library BLMs **(K–2)**; On My Way Practice Readers **(K–2)** CD-ROMs: *Lexia Phonics Primary Intervention* **(K–2)**; *Get Set for Reading* **(1–6)**; *Curious George Learns Phonics* **(K–2)**	
Structural Analysis/Phonics	TE: Monitoring Student Progress Phonics/Decoding Screening Test **(1–6)** *Lexia Quick Phonics Assessment CD-ROM* **(K–6)**	TE, Resources: Reteaching Lessons for Structural Analysis Skills **(3–6)** Other Reading: Leveled Readers Theme Paperbacks (below level) **(K–6)** CD-ROMs: *Get Set for Reading* **(1–6)**; *Lexia Phonics Intermediate Intervention* **(3–6)**	TE, Resources: Challenge/Extension Activities for Phonics **(1–2)** Other Reading: Theme Paperbacks (above level), Classroom Bookshelf **(K–6)** CD-ROM: *Wacky Web Tales* **(3–6)**
High-Frequency Words	TE: Monitoring Student Progress Leveled Reading Passages **(K–6)**	TE: High-Frequency Word Practice in Word Work sections **(K–2)** TE, Resources: Reteaching Lessons for High-Frequency Words **(1–2)** Other Reading: On My Way Practice Readers **(K)**, Phonics Library BLMs **(K–2)**	TE, Resources: Challenge/Extension Activities for High-Frequency Words **(1–2)** Other Reading: Little Big Books **(K–2)**, Classroom Bookshelf **(K–6)**
Reading Strategies	Observation Checklists Anecdotal Records Oral Reading Record Selection Tests **(2–6)** Leveled Reading Passages **(K–6)**	TE, each selection: Extra Support/Intervention boxes **(1–6)** TE: Strategy **(K)**; Strategy Focus, Extra Support/Intervention Strategy Modeling boxes **(1–6)**; Strategy Review, Strategy/Skill Preview **(3–6)** Big Books **(1–2)** PB: Strategy Poster **(1–6)** *Extra Support Handbook* (Phonics Decoding Strategy) **(K–6)**	TE, each selection: Challenge boxes **(1)** Other Reading: Theme Paperbacks (above level) **(1–6)**, Classroom Bookshelf **(1–6)**

If you want to assess...	You can use...	Then you can...	
		give extra support	**challenge**
Comprehension/ Comparing Texts	Observation checklists Anecdotal Records TE: Diagnostic Checks TE: Comprehension Checks Retellings and Summaries Selection Tests **(2–6)** Portfolio review Leveled Reading Passages Assessment Kit **(K–6)**	TE: Retelling or Summarizing prompts in Responding section **(K)**; Building Background **(K–6)**; Key Concepts **(K–3)** TE, each selection: Extra Support/Intervention boxes, Writing Support for Responding, Previewing the Text boxes **(1–6)**, Review Comprehension Lessons **(2–6)** TE, Resources: Reteaching Lessons for Comprehension Skills **(1–6)** TRB: Selection Summaries **(1–6)** Other Reading: On My Way Practice Readers, Phonics Library BLMs **(K–2)**; Reader's Library BLMs **(3–6)**; Theme Paperbacks (below level) **(1–6)**, CD-ROM: *Get Set for Reading* **(1–6)** Anthology Audios **(1–6)** *Extra Support Handbook* **(1–6)**	TE: Center Activities in Responding section **(K)** TE, each selection: Challenge boxes **(K–6)** and Assignment Cards **(2–6)**; Responding questions and activities **(K–2)** TE, Resources: Challenge/Extension Activities for Comprehension **(1–6)** Other Reading: Little Big Books **(K–2)**, Classroom Bookshelf **(K–6)**, Theme Paperbacks (above level) **(1–6)** *Challenge Handbook* **(K–6)**
Vocabulary	Selection Tests **(2–6)** Observation Checklists **(2–6)** Portfolio review	TE, each selection: Developing Key Vocabulary, Vocabulary boxes **(2–6)**	TE, Vocabulary Expansion **(1–2)**, Language Center: Vocabulary **(3–6)** TE, Resources: Challenge/Extension Activities for Vocabulary **(2–6)** CD-ROM: *Wacky Web Tales* **(1–6)**
Oral Reading Fluency	Observation Checklists Anecdotal records Oral Reading Record	TE, each selection: Fluency Practice Notes Other Reading: On My Way Practice Readers,	Other Reading: Theme Paperbacks (above level), Classroom Bookshelf **(1–6)**

If you want to assess...	You can use...	Then you can...	
		give extra support	**challenge**
Oral Reading Fluency (continued)	Leveled Reading Passages **(K–6)**	Phonics Library BLMs **(K–2)**; Theme Paperbacks (below level) **(1–6)**; Classroom Bookshelf (below level) **(K–6)**	
Response to Literature	Selection Tests **(2–6)** Observation Checklists Anecdotal records Portfolio review Student-teacher conferences	TE: Supporting Comprehension questions, Responding activities **(K–6)**; Writer's Craft lessons, Genre lessons **(1–6)**	TE, Focus on Genre: Responding activities, additional reading
Spelling	Phonics/Decoding Screening Test **(1–6)**	TE, each selection: Basic Words, Extra Support/Intervention box in Spelling Lesson **(1–6)**	TE, each selection: Challenge Words, Challenge box in Spelling Lesson **(1–6)**
Writing	Inventories Observation Checklists Anecdotal records Portfolio review Student-teacher conferences	TE: Shared, Interactive Independent Writing **(K)** TE, Reading-Writing Workshop: Student Writing Model, Writing Traits notes, Student Self-Assessment **(1–6)**	TE, each selection: Journal Writing, Genre lessons, Writer's Craft lessons **(1–6)** TE, Resources: Writing Activities **(2–6)** *Challenge Handbook* **(K–6)**
Grammar	TE: Monitoring Student Progress Portfolio review	TE: Grammar Review Lessons **(1)** TE, Resources: Reteaching Lessons for Grammar Skills **(2–6)** *Extra Support Handbook* **(3–6)**	CD-ROM: *Wacky Web Tales* **(3–6)**
Listening, Speaking, Viewing	Observation Checklists Anecdotal records	TE: Teacher Read Aloud, Listening/Speaking/ Viewing **(2–6)**	TE: Listening/Speaking/ Viewing **(2–6)**
English Language Proficiency	Checklists in Part 10 and in *Handbook for English Language Learners*	*Handbook for English Language Learners*	*Handbook for English Language Learners*

Evaluating Writing

Rubrics and Student Writing

Many teachers use rubrics to help them carefully evaluate student writing—and to help them teach students the elements of good writing. A scoring rubric shows the criteria by which an assignment will be evaluated and a number score for each criterion or set of criteria. Scoring rubrics also help teachers score student papers consistently. Whether they are used for scoring or not, however, rubrics can help students to know what to strive for in their writing and teachers to know what to look for in their students' work.

RUBRICS FOR EVALUATING DIFFERENT TYPES OF WRITING

Writing rubrics can be general—representing the elements of all good writing—or they can relate to a specific writing mode or type: description, story, research report, and so on. When you give a specific writing assignment, it helps for students to see your evaluation rubric early in the writing process so that they understand the criteria you will use to evaluate their work. Your students will also benefit from seeing one or more writing samples that exemplify each set of criteria and score on a rubric—particularly an example of an outstanding paper.

RUBRICS FOR SCORING WRITTEN RESPONSES ON TESTS

You can adapt or create rubrics for scoring test responses, but keep in mind that "on-demand" writing is typically less polished than writing-process writing. Rubrics for on-demand writing should stress content over form and polish. Although students should use prewriting techniques to tackle longer essay questions, they won't have the benefit of peer or student-teacher conferences, relatively unlimited time for full revising and proofreading stages, and access to reference books.

Holistic Scoring

Holistic scoring is based on the idea that the success of a piece of writing depends on how well all its parts (content, organization, language, conventions, and so on) act together to communicate ideas and information. Holistic scoring rubrics may be general or specific to writing types.

Program Resources

- Each theme's Reading-Writing Workshop (Grades 1–6) begins with a complete student model of the writing type taught in the workshop, and the *Teacher's Edition* includes a scoring rubric.

- The Teacher's Annotated Editions of the *Integrated Theme Tests* (K–6) and the *Benchmark Progress Tests* include scoring rubrics for open-response comprehension questions and scoring rubrics and anchor papers for compositions written in response to prompts.

· Houghton Mifflin ·
Reading

Holistic scoring is used not only in classroom evaluation of writing but also in large-scale proficiency testing. Your district or state may use a holistic scoring rubric to evaluate student performance. If so, you may want to use that rubric so that students can become familiar with it. Otherwise, you may want to use the mode-specific scoring rubrics in HOUGHTON MIFFLIN READING.

Beginning at Level 1.3, the Reading-Writing Workshop for each theme contains a holistic writing traits scoring rubric for evaluating the type of writing taught in that workshop; see the chart on page 38 for a list of writing types and their respective locations. Four-point rubrics are easy to use and sufficient for many teachers' needs. A general four-point holistic writing traits scoring rubric is shown on page 39. Some states and districts require a six-point writing traits rubric, however, so included is one general six-point rubric, followed by six-point rubrics for all writing modes covered in the Reading-Writing Workshops. There are three sets of rubrics, one set each for Grades 1–2, 3–4, and 5–6. For ease of use, they are arranged first by grade and then in alphabetical order.

Alternatively, you may want to build your own holistic writing traits scoring rubric. Here is one way.

1. Decide the scale you want to use. (Four-point and six-point scales are used most often.)

2. Determine the qualities for a top-scoring composition based on the key characteristics or writing traits you want to evaluate. Write the descriptor for that level of performance.

3. Then describe how those same traits appear at each lower level of performance. It is important that students be able to understand your scoring, accurately self-assess, and revise where appropriate.

"I like to climb a tree"
When the sun comes out
I like to shout.
I like to climb a tree
to see what I can see.

SCORING RUBRICS BY MODE IN HOUGHTON MIFFLIN READING

Level	Mode	Theme	Page
1.3	Personal Narrative	Home Sweet Home	T105
1.3	Description	Animal Adventures	T99
1.4	Story	We Can Work It Out	T99
1.4	Research Report	Our Earth	T97
1.5	Friendly Letter	Special Friends	T101
1.5	Instructions	We Can Do It!	T103
2.1	Story	Silly Stories	T95
2.1	Description	Nature Walk	T101
2.1	Friendly Letter	Around Town	T101
2.2	Research Report	Amazing Animals	T105
2.2	Personal Narrative	Family Time	T99
2.2	Instructions	Talent Show	T103
3.1	Personal Narrative	Off to Adventure!	51H
3.1	Instructions	Celebrating Traditions	187H
3.1	Story	Incredible Stories	335H
3.2	Research Report	Animal Habitats	43H
3.2	Description	Voyagers	185H
3.2	Persuasive Essay	Smart Solutions	339H
4	Personal Narrative	Journeys	59H
4	Description	American Stories	183H
4	Story	That's Amazing!	325H
4	Persuasive Essay	Problem Solvers	413H
4	Personal Essay	Heroes	557H
4	Research Report	Nature: Friend and Foe	657H
5	Description	Nature's Fury	53H
5	Personal Essay	Give It All You've Got	159H
5	Story	Voices of the Revolution	289H
5	Personal Narrative	Person to Person	365H
5	Research Report	One Land, Many Trails	495H
5	Persuasive Essay	Animal Encounters	625H
6	Personal Narrative	Courage	49H
6	Story	What Really Happened?	167H
6	Description	Growing Up	273H
6	Research Report	Discovering Ancient Cultures	387H
6	Personal Essay	Doers and Dreamers	475H
6	Persuasive Essay	New Frontiers: Oceans and Space	571H

4

Ideas: The paper clearly focuses on the topic and the purpose. **Organization:** Strong main ideas and exact details are grouped logically in paragraphs. Paragraphs are ordered in a logical sequence. **Voice:** The writer's voice is strong. **Word Choice:** The paper uses many vivid, exact words. **Sentence Fluency:** The sentences exhibit good variety and flow smoothly. **Conventions:** There are few, if any, mistakes. **Presentation:** The final copy is neat and legible.

3

Ideas: The paper mostly focuses on the topic and the purpose. Some ideas or details may be weak, or more details are needed. **Organization:** The organization is generally clear, but the beginning or the ending could be stronger. **Voice:** The writer's voice could be stronger. **Word Choice:** Additional exact words are needed. **Sentence Fluency:** The paper needs more sentence variety. **Conventions:** Mistakes do not affect understanding. **Presentation:** The final copy may be a bit messy but is legible.

2

Ideas: Much of the paper is not clearly focused. There may be few ideas, or the ideas may be unimportant. There are few details. **Organization:** The organization is confused. The beginning or ending may be missing. **Voice:** The writer's voice may be weak. **Word Choice:** Word choice is inexact or repetitive. **Sentence Fluency:** The paper lacks sentence variety. **Conventions:** Mistakes sometimes make the paper confusing. **Presentation:** The final copy may be messy.

1

Ideas: The paper may not be focused on one topic and purpose. There are no details, or they are unimportant. **Organization:** The ideas are disorganized or are simply presented as a list. **Voice:** The paper lacks voice. **Word Choice:** Word choice is inexact and uninteresting. **Sentence Fluency:** Sentences are short or repetitive. **Conventions:** Many mistakes make the paper confusing. **Presentation:** The final copy is messy and often illegible.

General Holistic Writing Traits Scoring Rubric

6

Ideas: The paper clearly focuses on the topic and the purpose. **Organization:** Strong main ideas and exact details are grouped logically in paragraphs. Paragraphs are ordered in a logical sequence. **Voice:** The writer's voice is strong. **Word Choice:** The paper uses many vivid, exact words. **Sentence Fluency:** The sentences exhibit good variety and flow smoothly. **Conventions:** There are few, if any, mistakes. **Presentation:** The final copy is neat and legible.

5

Ideas: The paper focuses on the topic and the purpose. The topic is well supported by several good main ideas and details, but more details would be helpful. **Organization:** Ideas and details are grouped in paragraphs in a logical order. **Voice:** The writer's voice is fairly strong. **Word Choice:** More exact words would be helpful. **Sentence Fluency:** Sentences sound natural. There is good variety. **Conventions:** There are few errors. **Presentation:** The final copy is generally neat and legible.

4

Ideas: The paper mostly focuses on the topic and the purpose. Some ideas or details may be weak, or more details are needed. **Organization:** The organization is generally clear, but the beginning or the ending may be weak. **Voice:** The writer's voice could be stronger. **Word Choice:** Additional exact words are needed. **Sentence Fluency:** The paper needs more sentence variety. **Conventions:** Mistakes do not affect understanding. **Presentation:** The final copy may be a bit messy but is legible.

3

Ideas: The paper mostly focuses on the topic and the purpose. Some ideas may be unimportant, or important ideas and details are missing. **Organization:** Some organization is evident. The beginning or ending is weak or missing. **Voice:** The writer's voice is somewhat weak. **Word Choice:** Word choice is vague or uninteresting. **Sentence Fluency:** The paper shows little sentence variety. **Conventions:** There may be many mistakes. **Presentation:** The final copy may be somewhat difficult to read.

2

Ideas: Much of the paper is not clearly focused. There may be few ideas, or the ideas may be unimportant. There are very few details. **Organization:** The organization is confused. The beginning or ending may be missing. **Voice:** The writer's voice may be weak. **Word Choice:** Word choice is inexact or repetitive. **Sentence Fluency:** The paper lacks sentence variety. **Conventions:** Mistakes sometimes make the paper confusing. **Presentation:** The final copy may be messy.

1

Ideas: The paper may not be focused on one topic and purpose. There are no details, or they are unimportant. **Organization:** The ideas are disorganized or are simply presented as a list. **Voice:** The paper lacks voice. **Word Choice:** Word choice is inexact and uninteresting. **Sentence Fluency:** Sentences are short or repetitive. **Conventions:** Many mistakes make the paper confusing. **Presentation:** The final copy is messy and often illegible.

6

Ideas: The description focuses on a single, clear topic. Details tell what the writer saw, heard, tasted, smelled, or felt. **Organization:** The details are presented in a clear order. **Voice:** The writer clearly expresses his or her feelings. **Word Choice:** Many exact sensory words create a vivid picture. **Sentence Fluency:** The writing flows well. Sentences vary in length and structure. **Conventions:** There are few, if any, errors. **Presentation:** The final copy is neat and legible.

5

Ideas: The description focuses on a single, clear topic. Details are vivid, but a few more would be beneficial. **Organization:** The organization is generally clear. **Voice:** The writer's voice is evident. **Word Choice:** Sensory words help create a vivid picture, but more are needed. **Sentence Fluency:** Sentences are varied and flow well. **Conventions:** There are few errors. **Presentation:** The final copy is generally neat and legible.

4

Ideas: The description mostly focuses on a topic, but it needs more details that address at least three of the five senses. **Organization:** The organization could be improved. **Voice:** The writer's voice could be stronger. **Word Choice:** Additional exact sensory words are needed. **Sentence Fluency:** More sentence variety is needed. **Conventions:** Mistakes do not affect understanding. **Presentation:** The final copy is a bit messy but legible.

3

Ideas: The description generally focuses on one topic. The paper needs many more details that address at least three of the five senses. **Organization:** The organization may be somewhat random. **Voice:** The writer's voice is somewhat weak. **Word Choice:** The description needs many more exact sensory words. **Sentence Fluency:** Sentences lack variety. **Conventions:** There may be many mistakes. **Presentation:** The final copy may be messy and hard to read.

2

Ideas: The description may not clearly focus on one topic. There are few details and they are imprecise. **Organization:** Details are not ordered clearly. **Voice:** The writer's voice is weak or missing. **Word Choice:** Few exact sensory words are used. Vocabulary is limited. **Sentence Fluency:** Sentences are short or repetitive. **Conventions:** Mistakes sometimes make the paper confusing. **Presentation:** The final copy is messy. It may be illegible in a few places.

1

Ideas: The description is not focused. There are no details, or they are inappropriate. **Organization:** Details are disorganized. The description rambles. **Voice:** The writer's voice is missing. **Word Choice:** Few, if any, sensory words are used. Word choice is vague or uninteresting. **Sentence Fluency:** There are few sentences, or they are very short, unclear, or incomplete. **Conventions:** Many mistakes make the paper hard to understand. **Presentation:** The final copy is messy and often illegible.

Grades 1–2 Writing Traits Scoring Rubric: Friendly Letter

6

Ideas: The writer tells enough information to answer questions the reader might have. **Organization:** The writer included all five letter parts correctly. Information is presented in a clear order. **Voice:** The writer writes in a lively way that conveys his or her feelings. **Word Choice:** The writer uses many exact words. **Sentence Fluency:** The writing flows well. Sentences vary in length and structure. **Conventions:** There are few, if any, errors. **Presentation:** The final copy is neat and legible.

5

Ideas: The writer tells interesting information, but a few more details would be helpful. **Organization:** The writer included all five letter parts. Information is presented in a generally clear order. **Voice:** The writer's voice is evident. **Word Choice:** The writer uses exact words, but more would be desirable. **Sentence Fluency:** Sentences are varied and flow well. **Conventions:** There are few errors. **Presentation:** The final copy is generally neat and legible.

4

Ideas: The writer includes details, but more are needed. **Organization:** One of the five parts may be missing or may be used incorrectly. A few details may be misplaced in the body of the letter. **Voice:** The writer's voice could be stronger. **Word Choice:** Word choice sometimes causes confusion. **Sentence Fluency:** More sentence variety is needed. **Conventions:** Mistakes do not affect understanding. **Presentation:** The final copy is a bit messy but is legible.

3

Ideas: The writer includes some details, but many more are needed. **Organization:** The writer may not have included several parts of the letter or may have used them incorrectly. The body of the letter is somewhat confusing. **Voice:** The writer's voice is somewhat weak. **Word Choice:** Many more exact words are needed. **Sentence Fluency:** Sentences lack variety. **Conventions:** There are many mistakes. **Presentation:** The final copy may be messy and hard to read.

2

Ideas: The writer provides very few details. **Organization:** The paper is a letter but is missing several parts or uses them incorrectly. The presentation of information is random or confusing. **Voice:** The writer's voice is weak or missing. **Word Choice:** The words are unclear or confusing. **Sentence Fluency:** Sentences are short or repetitive. **Conventions:** Mistakes sometimes make the letter confusing. **Presentation:** The final copy is messy. It may be illegible in a few places.

1

Ideas: There are no details about the topic, or they are inappropriate. **Organization:** The paper is not in letter format. All five parts are missing. Information is disorganized. **Voice:** The writer's voice is missing. **Word Choice:** The words are confusing or general. **Sentence Fluency:** There are few sentences, or they are very short, unclear, or incomplete. **Conventions:** Many mistakes make the paper hard to understand. **Presentation:** The final copy is messy and often illegible.

6

Ideas: The paper focuses on one set of instructions. The instructions include all materials and specific details so that each step is clear, complete, and easy to follow. **Organization:** Steps and information are presented in order, using many time-order words. **Voice:** The writing grabs the reader's attention. **Word Choice:** The writer uses many exact verbs. **Sentence Fluency:** The writing flows well. Sentences vary in length and structure. **Conventions:** There are few, if any, errors. **Presentation:** The final copy is neat and legible.

5

Ideas: The instructions include the important materials and details. **Organization:** Steps are presented in order. The writer uses time-order words, although a few more would be beneficial. **Voice:** The writing is interesting. **Word Choice:** The writer uses exact verbs, but more might be helpful. **Sentence Fluency:** Sentences are varied and flow well. **Conventions:** There are few errors. **Presentation:** The final copy is generally neat and legible.

4

Ideas: The instructions include the important materials and steps, but more details are needed. **Organization:** The steps are mostly in order, but the sequence may not always be clear. More time-order words are needed. **Voice:** The writing could be more interesting. **Word Choice:** Additional exact verbs would improve clarity. **Sentence Fluency:** More sentence variety is needed. **Conventions:** Mistakes do not affect understanding. **Presentation:** The final copy is a bit messy but is legible.

3

Ideas: The instructions are not clearly focused. Some materials and steps are missing. **Organization:** The order of steps may cause some confusion or problems. More time-order words are needed. **Voice:** The writing rarely engages the reader's attention. **Word Choice:** Many more exact verbs are needed for clarity. **Sentence Fluency:** Sentences lack variety. **Conventions:** There may be many mistakes. **Presentation:** The final copy may be messy and hard to read.

2

Ideas: The instructions are not focused. Many materials are missing, or many steps and details are missing or unclear. **Organization:** The sequence is unclear and confusing. **Voice:** The writing is not engaging. **Word Choice:** Word choice is limited and repetitive. Verbs are vague. **Sentence Fluency:** Sentences are short or repetitive. **Conventions:** Mistakes sometimes make the instructions confusing. **Presentation:** The final copy is messy. It may be illegible in a few places.

1

Ideas: The paper is unfocused. Most materials, steps, and details are missing. **Organization:** The instructions are disorganized and confusing. Ideas may simply be listed. **Voice:** The writing is flat. **Word Choice:** Word choice is inexact and confusing. **Sentence Fluency:** There are few sentences, or they are very short, unclear, or incomplete. **Conventions:** Many mistakes make the instructions hard to understand. **Presentation:** The final copy is messy and often illegible.

Grades 1–2 Writing Traits Scoring Rubric: Personal Narrative

6

Ideas: The narrative focuses on a single experience. Many details create a vivid picture. **Organization:** The beginning catches the reader's interest. Events are told in order. A good ending wraps up the narrative. **Voice:** The writer clearly conveys his or her feelings. **Word Choice:** The writer uses interesting and exact words. **Sentence Fluency:** The writing flows well. Sentences vary in length and structure. **Conventions:** There are few, if any, errors. **Presentation:** The final copy is neat and legible.

5

Ideas: The narrative focuses on a single experience. Details create a clear picture, although more would be desirable. **Organization:** The order of events is clear. The narrative has a good beginning and ending. **Voice:** The writer expresses his or her feelings. **Word Choice:** The writer uses interesting and exact words, although more are needed. **Sentence Fluency:** Sentences are varied and flow well. **Conventions:** There are few errors. **Presentation:** The final copy is generally neat and legible.

4

Ideas: The narrative focuses on one experience, but there may be extraneous information. Additional details are needed. **Organization:** Some details may be out of order. The beginning may be dull or the ending abrupt. **Voice:** The writer's voice could be stronger. **Word Choice:** The language needs to be more exact and interesting. **Sentence Fluency:** More sentence variety is needed. **Conventions:** Mistakes do not affect understanding. **Presentation:** The final copy is a bit messy but is legible.

3

Ideas: The narrative focuses on one experience, but it includes much extraneous information or lacks many details. **Organization:** The sequence of events is somewhat confusing. The beginning or the ending may be weak or missing. **Voice:** The writer's voice is somewhat weak. **Word Choice:** The language is limited and inexact. **Sentence Fluency:** Sentences lack variety. **Conventions:** There may be many mistakes. **Presentation:** The final copy may be messy and hard to read.

2

Ideas: The narrative often loses focus. There are few details. **Organization:** The order of events is confusing or random. The beginning or the ending may be weak or missing. **Voice:** The writer's voice is weak or missing. **Word Choice:** Language is inexact or confusing. **Sentence Fluency:** Sentences are short or repetitive. **Conventions:** Mistakes sometimes make the narrative confusing. **Presentation:** The final copy is messy. It may be illegible in a few places.

1

Ideas: The narrative is unfocused or lacks details. **Organization:** Events are told randomly. It is hard to understand what happened. There is no beginning or ending. **Voice:** The narrative lacks voice. **Word Choice:** Language is vague or confusing. **Sentence Fluency:** There are few sentences, or they are very short, unclear, or incomplete. **Conventions:** Many mistakes make the narrative hard to understand. **Presentation:** The final copy is messy and often illegible.

6

Ideas: The report focuses on a specific topic. The writer includes many interesting facts about the topic. **Organization:** Facts are well organized. The ending wraps up the report. **Voice:** The writer uses his or her own words. **Word Choice:** The writer uses many exact words so that the information is clear. **Sentence Fluency:** The writing flows well. Sentences vary in length and structure. **Conventions:** There are few, if any, errors. **Presentation:** The final copy is neat and legible.

5

Ideas: The report focuses on a topic. The writer includes interesting facts about the topic, although a few more would be beneficial. **Organization:** Facts are mostly well organized. The report has a satisfactory ending. **Voice:** The writer uses his or her own words. **Word Choice:** The writer uses exact words. **Sentence Fluency:** Sentences are varied and flow well. **Conventions:** There are few errors. **Presentation:** The final copy is generally neat and legible.

4

Ideas: The report mostly focuses on the topic. More facts are needed. **Organization:** Some facts may be out of order. The ending may not wrap up the report. **Voice:** The writer mostly used his or her own words. **Word Choice:** Word choice could be more exact so that facts are clearer. **Sentence Fluency:** More sentence variety is needed. **Conventions:** Mistakes do not affect understanding. **Presentation:** The final copy is a bit messy but is legible.

3

Ideas: The report generally focuses on the topic. Many more facts are needed. **Organization:** Facts are not clearly organized. The ending may be weak or missing. **Voice:** The writer often relies on phrasing from the sources. **Word Choice:** Word choice is often inexact, and information is often unclear. **Sentence Fluency:** Sentences lack variety. **Conventions:** There may be many mistakes. **Presentation:** The final copy may be messy and hard to read.

2

Ideas: The report may not focus on a clear topic. There are few facts. **Organization:** Facts are out of order. The report ends abruptly. **Voice:** The writer mostly does not use his or her own words. **Word Choice:** Words are inexact, and facts are unclear. **Sentence Fluency:** Sentences are short or repetitive. **Conventions:** Mistakes sometimes make the report confusing. **Presentation:** The final copy is messy. It may be illegible in a few places.

1

Ideas: The report lacks focus. There are almost no facts. No research may have been done. **Organization:** Information is disorganized, unclear, or simply listed. **Voice:** The writer copied the paper from sources. **Word Choice:** Word choice is vague and limited. **Sentence Fluency:** There are few sentences, or they are very short, unclear, or incomplete. **Conventions:** Many mistakes make the report hard to understand. **Presentation:** The final copy is messy and often illegible.

Grades 1–2 Writing Traits Scoring Rubric: Story

6

Ideas: There are many details about the character(s) and the problem. An interesting title tells what the story is about. **Organization:** The story has a clear beginning, middle, and end. **Voice:** The writer wrote in a lively way that engages the reader's attention. **Word Choice:** The writer uses many exact, descriptive words. **Sentence Fluency:** The writing flows well. Sentences vary in length and structure. **Conventions:** There are few, if any, errors. **Presentation:** The final copy is neat and legible.

5

Ideas: Details tell about the character(s) and the problem, but more details would be helpful. The story has a good title. **Organization:** The story has a beginning, middle, and end. **Voice:** The writer tells the story in an interesting way. **Word Choice:** The writer uses some exact, descriptive words. **Sentence Fluency:** Sentences are varied and flow well. **Conventions:** There are few errors. **Presentation:** The final copy is generally neat and legible.

4

Ideas: More details are needed about the characters and the problem. The title is appropriate but boring. **Organization:** The beginning, middle, or end may be confusing or out of order. **Voice:** The writer sometimes engages the reader's attention. **Word Choice:** Word choice could be more exact and descriptive. **Sentence Fluency:** More sentence variety is needed. **Conventions:** Mistakes do not affect understanding. **Presentation:** The final copy is a bit messy but is legible.

3

Ideas: Many more details are needed about the characters and the problem. The title is boring. **Organization:** The beginning, middle, or end may be confusing or missing. **Voice:** The writing rarely engages the reader's attention. **Word Choice:** Word choice is inexact and limited. **Sentence Fluency:** Sentences lack variety. **Conventions:** There are many mistakes. **Presentation:** The final copy may be messy and hard to read.

2

Ideas: The story may lack a problem. There are few details. The title is weak or missing. **Organization:** The beginning, the middle, or the end may be missing. **Voice:** The writing is not engaging. **Word Choice:** The words chosen are vague and uninteresting. **Sentence Fluency:** Sentences are short or repetitive. **Conventions:** Mistakes sometimes make the story confusing. **Presentation:** The final copy is messy. It may be illegible in a few places.

1

Ideas: There are no details. It is unclear who the characters are and what is happening, or there is no story. There is no title. **Organization:** There is no beginning or ending. **Voice:** The writing is flat. **Word Choice:** Word choice is inexact and repetitive. **Sentence Fluency:** There are few sentences, or they are very short, unclear, or incomplete. **Conventions:** Many mistakes make the paper hard to understand. **Presentation:** The final copy is messy and often illegible.

Grades 3–4 Writing Traits Scoring Rubric: Description

6

Ideas: The description focuses on one topic, using many vivid, interesting details. **Organization:** Details are well organized. An interesting beginning introduces the topic. A good ending wraps up the description. **Voice:** The writer's voice is strong. **Word Choice:** Many exact, sensory words create a vivid picture. **Sentence Fluency:** Sentences exhibit interesting variety and flow smoothly. **Conventions:** There are few, if any, errors. **Presentation:** The final copy is neat and legible.

5

Ideas: The writer uses vivid details to describe a clear topic. **Organization:** Details are generally well organized. The beginning introduces the topic. The ending wraps up the description. **Voice:** The writer's voice is evident. **Word Choice:** Exact, sensory words create a clear picture, but more would be beneficial. **Sentence Fluency:** Sentences sound natural, and there is good variety. **Conventions:** There are few errors. **Presentation:** The final copy is generally neat and legible.

4

Ideas: The description focuses on a topic, but more vivid details are needed. **Organization:** The organization is generally clear. The beginning and the ending may be somewhat weak. **Voice:** The writer's voice could be stronger. **Word Choice:** The writer could have used more exact words and more sensory words. **Sentence Fluency:** The paper needs greater sentence variety. **Conventions:** Mistakes do not affect understanding. **Presentation:** The final copy may be a bit messy but is legible.

3

Ideas: The description focuses on a topic but may contain extraneous details. Many more details are needed. **Organization:** Details are somewhat organized. The beginning and the ending may be weak. **Voice:** The writer's voice is weak. **Word Choice:** The paper needs many more exact, sensory words. **Sentence Fluency:** The paper shows little sentence variety. **Conventions:** There may be a number of mistakes. **Presentation:** The final copy may be somewhat difficult to read.

2

Ideas: The description may not be clearly focused on a topic. Few details are included. **Organization:** Details are not organized. The beginning and ending are weak or missing. **Voice:** The writer's voice is weak or missing. **Word Choice:** The writer uses few exact words or sensory words. **Sentence Fluency:** The paper lacks sentence variety. **Conventions:** Mistakes sometimes make the paper hard to understand. **Presentation:** The final copy may be messy and hard to read.

1

Ideas: The description may not be focused. There are no details, or they are inappropriate. **Organization:** Details are unorganized. The beginning and ending are missing. **Voice:** The paper lacks voice. **Word Choice:** Word choice is vague or uninteresting. It may be confusing. **Sentence Fluency:** Sentences are very short, unclear, or repetitive. **Conventions:** Many mistakes make the paper hard to understand. **Presentation:** The final copy is messy. It may be illegible in many places.

Grade 3 Writing Traits Scoring Rubric: Instructions

6

Ideas: The paper focuses on one set of instructions, includes all necessary materials and steps, and provides many exact details. **Organization:** An interesting beginning tells the topic. The steps are in order with many order words. **Voice:** The writing holds the reader's attention. **Word Choice:** The writer uses many precise words. **Sentence Fluency:** Sentence exhibit interesting variety and flow smoothly. **Conventions:** There are few, if any, errors. **Presentation:** The final copy is neat and legible.

5

Ideas: The paper focuses on a set of instructions, includes the important materials and steps, and provides exact details. **Organization:** The beginning tells the topic. The steps are in order. More order words would be helpful. **Voice:** The writing usually holds the reader's attention. **Word Choice:** The writer uses precise words, but more would be helpful. **Sentence Fluency:** Sentences sound natural, and there is good variety. **Conventions:** There are few errors. **Presentation:** The final copy is generally neat and legible.

4

Ideas: The paper presents the important materials and steps for a set of instructions. More details are needed. **Organization:** The beginning may be uninteresting. The steps are in order, but more order words are needed. **Voice:** The writing sometimes holds the reader's attention. **Word Choice:** Additional exact words are needed. **Sentence Fluency:** The paper shows little sentence variety. **Conventions:** Mistakes do not affect understanding. **Presentation:** The final copy may be a bit messy but is legible.

3

Ideas: The paper focuses on a set of instructions, but the materials and steps are incomplete and sometimes confusing. **Organization:** Steps are not clearly ordered and may cause confusion. The beginning is uninteresting or missing. **Voice:** The writing rarely holds the reader's attention. **Word Choice:** Many more exact words are needed. **Sentence Fluency:** The paper needs greater sentence variety. **Conventions:** Three may be a number of mistakes. **Presentation:** The final copy may be somewhat difficult to read.

2

Ideas: The paper may not focus on one topic. Important materials and steps are missing. Details are missing or unclear. **Organization:** The beginning is missing. Steps are not in order. Order words are needed. **Voice:** The writing does not hold the reader's attention. **Word Choice:** Word choice is inexact or limited. **Sentence Fluency:** The paper lacks sentence variety. **Conventions:** Mistakes sometimes make the instructions hard to understand. **Presentation:** The final copy may be messy and hard to read.

1

Ideas: The paper may not clearly focus on a topic. The instructions cannot be followed because important information is missing. **Organization:** The paper lacks organization or is simply a list. **Voice:** The writing is flat. **Word Choice:** Word choice is vague or repetitive. It may be confusing. **Sentence Fluency:** Sentences are very short, unclear, or repetitive. **Conventions:** Many mistakes make the paper hard to understand. **Presentation:** The final copy is messy and often illegible.

Grade 4 Writing Traits Scoring Rubric: Personal Essay

6

Ideas: The essay supports an opinion with several good reasons and specific details. **Organization:** Ideas are presented in well-organized paragraphs. An interesting introduction states the opinion and the conclusion summarizes it. **Voice:** The writer's voice is strong. **Word Choice:** Words are precise, active, and descriptive. **Sentence Fluency:** Sentences exhibit interesting variety and flow smoothly. **Conventions:** There are few, if any, errors. **Presentation:** The final copy is neat and legible.

5

Ideas: The essay supports an opinion with reasons and details, although more details would be helpful. **Organization:** Reasons and details are organized in paragraphs. The introduction and conclusion are appropriate. **Voice:** The writer's voice is evident. **Word Choice:** Language is interesting and exact, but additional exact words are needed. **Sentence Fluency:** Sentences sound natural, and there is good variety. **Conventions:** There are few errors. **Presentation:** The final copy is generally neat and legible.

4

Ideas: Several reasons support an opinion, but one reason may be weak. More details are needed. **Organization:** The introduction or conclusion may be boring. Some parts could be better developed or organized. **Voice:** The writer's voice could be stronger. **Word Choice:** More exact, interesting words are needed. **Sentence Fluency:** The essay needs greater sentence variety. **Conventions:** Mistakes do not affect understanding. **Presentation:** The final copy may be a bit messy but is legible.

3

Ideas: The essay focuses on an opinion, but it needs more or stronger reasons. Many additional details are needed. **Organization:** The introduction or conclusion may be weak. Many parts are not well developed or organized. **Voice:** The writer's voice may be weak. **Word Choice:** Language is inexact or boring. **Sentence Fluency:** The essay shows little sentence variety. **Conventions:** There may be many mistakes. **Presentation:** The final copy may be somewhat difficult to read.

2

Ideas: The essay sometimes loses focus. Reasons and details are weak. **Organization:** The introduction or conclusion may be missing. Ideas are poorly organized. **Voice:** The writer's voice may be missing or weak. **Word Choice:** Word choice is limited and repetitive. **Sentence Fluency:** The essay lacks sentence variety. **Conventions:** Mistakes sometimes make the essay hard to understand. **Presentation:** The final copy may be messy and hard to read.

1

Ideas: The essay may not focus on an opinion or express several opinions with little support. **Organization:** Ideas are unorganized or just listed. **Voice:** The writing is flat. **Word Choice:** Word choice is vague or uninteresting. It may be confusing. **Sentence Fluency:** Sentences are very short, unclear, or repetitive. **Conventions:** Many mistakes make the essay hard to understand. **Presentation:** The final copy is messy and often illegible.

Grades 3–4 Writing Traits Scoring Rubric: Personal Narrative

6

Ideas: The narrative focuses on a single experience. Many well-chosen details tell what the writer saw, heard, tasted, smelled, and felt. **Organization:** The beginning catches the reader's interest. Events are told in a clear order. **Voice:** The writer expresses his or her personality. **Word Choice:** The writer uses numerous exact, interesting words. **Sentence Fluency:** Sentences exhibit interesting variety and flow smoothly. **Conventions:** There are few, if any, errors. **Presentation:** The final copy is neat and legible.

5

Ideas: The narrative focuses on a single experience. Details tell what the writer saw, heard, tasted, smelled, and felt. **Organization:** The beginning is good. The narrative is generally well organized. **Voice:** The writer's personality is evident. **Word Choice:** The writer uses exact, interesting words, although more would be desirable. **Sentence Fluency:** Sentences sound natural, and there is good variety. **Conventions:** There are few errors. **Presentation:** The final copy is generally neat and legible.

4

Ideas: The narrative generally focuses on one experience, but it may include extraneous information. More details are needed. **Organization:** The beginning could be more interesting. The order of events may be unclear. **Voice:** The writer's voice could be stronger. **Word Choice:** Additional exact words are needed. **Sentence Fluency:** The paper needs greater sentence variety. **Conventions:** Mistakes do not affect understanding. **Presentation:** The final copy may be a bit messy but is legible.

3

Ideas: The narrative has a clear topic but includes extraneous information. Many additional details are needed. **Organization:** The beginning may be weak or missing. The order of events may be unclear. **Voice:** The writer's voice is somewhat weak. **Word Choice:** Word choice may be repetitive or inexact. **Sentence Fluency:** The paper shows little sentence variety. **Conventions:** There may be a number of mistakes. **Presentation:** The final copy may be somewhat difficult to read.

2

Ideas: The narrative has a topic, but it lacks details or includes much extraneous information. **Organization:** The beginning is dull or missing. The order of events is confusing. **Voice:** The writer's voice is weak or missing. **Word Choice:** Word choice is limited and repetitive. **Sentence Fluency:** The narrative lacks sentence variety. **Conventions:** Mistakes sometimes make the paper hard to understand. **Presentation:** The final copy may be messy and hard to read.

1

Ideas: The narrative does not focus on one experience. There are few or no details. It is hard to understand what happened. **Organization:** There may be no clear beginning, middle, or end. **Voice:** The writer's voice is missing. **Word Choice:** Word choice is vague and repetitive throughout. **Sentence Fluency:** Sentences are very short, unclear, or repetitive. **Conventions:** Many mistakes make the paper hard to understand. **Presentation:** The final copy is messy and often illegible.

6

Ideas: The essay focuses on a clear goal supported by several strong reasons, facts, and examples. **Organization:** An interesting beginning states the goal. The support is organized into well-developed paragraphs. **Voice:** The voice is confident. The writer expresses feelings. **Word Choice:** The writer uses effective persuasive language. **Sentence Fluency:** Sentences exhibit interesting variety and flow smoothly. **Conventions:** There are few, if any, errors. **Presentation:** The final copy is neat and legible.

5

Ideas: The essay focuses on a goal supported by reasons, facts, and examples, although more support may be needed. **Organization:** The beginning states the goal. Reasons and supporting facts and examples are organized into paragraphs. **Voice:** The writer's voice is evident. **Word Choice:** The writer uses persuasive language. **Sentence Fluency:** Sentences sound natural, and there is good variety. **Conventions:** There are few errors. **Presentation:** The final copy is generally neat and legible.

4

Ideas: The essay focuses on a goal and supporting reasons, facts, and examples. More support is needed. **Organization:** A few facts and examples may be misplaced. The beginning may be boring. **Voice:** The writer's voice could be stronger. **Word Choice:** The essay needs more persuasive language. **Sentence Fluency:** The essay needs greater sentence variety. **Conventions:** Mistakes do not affect understanding. **Presentation:** The final copy may be a bit messy but is legible.

3

Ideas: The essay mostly focuses on a goal and supporting reasons, facts, and examples. The goal may be unclear, and the support may be weak. **Organization:** Supporting information may not be clearly organized. **Voice:** The writer's voice is somewhat weak. **Word Choice:** The essay has little persuasive language. **Sentence Fluency:** The essay shows little sentence variety. **Conventions:** There may be many mistakes. **Presentation:** The final copy may be somewhat difficult to read.

2

Ideas: The essay does not focus on a goal, or support is limited and unconvincing. **Organization:** The goal is not stated. Support is poorly organized. **Voice:** The writer's voice is weak or missing. **Word Choice:** Language is boring and unpersuasive. **Sentence Fluency:** The essay lacks sentence variety. **Conventions:** Mistakes sometimes make the essay hard to understand. **Presentation:** The final copy may be messy and hard to read.

1

Ideas: The goal is unclear. There is no support, or it is unconvincing. **Organization:** Ideas are unorganized or just listed. **Voice:** The voice is missing. **Word Choice:** Language is vague and unpersuasive. **Sentence Fluency:** Sentences are very short, unclear, or repetitive. **Conventions:** Many mistakes make the essay hard to understand. **Presentation:** The final copy is messy and often illegible.

Grades 3–4 Writing Traits Scoring Rubric: Research Report

6

Ideas: The paper is a well-researched, factual report about a clear topic with an accurate bibliography. **Organization:** Information is well organized into paragraphs with strong topic sentences, supporting facts and examples, an interesting beginning, and an effective conclusion. **Voice:** The writer uses his or her own words. **Word Choice:** Words are precise and descriptive. **Sentence Fluency:** Sentences exhibit good variety and flow smoothly. **Conventions:** There are few, if any, errors. **Presentation:** The final copy is neat and legible.

5

Ideas: The paper presents many facts about a clear topic. It has a good bibliography. **Organization:** Facts are grouped into paragraphs with topic sentences. It includes a good beginning and conclusion. **Voice:** The writer uses his or her own words. **Word Choice:** Words are exact. **Sentence Fluency:** Sentences sound natural. There is good variety. **Conventions:** There are few errors. **Presentation:** The final copy is generally neat and legible.

4

Ideas: More facts are needed. The bibliography may be incomplete. **Organization:** More topic sentences are needed. Facts may not be well organized. The conclusion may be weak. **Voice:** The writer mostly uses his or her own words. **Word Choice:** More exact words are needed. **Sentence Fluency:** The report needs more sentence variety. **Conventions:** Mistakes do not affect understanding. **Presentation:** The final copy may be a bit messy but is legible.

3

Ideas: The report is not clearly focused. More facts are needed. The bibliography may be incomplete. **Organization:** Topic sentences are missing or weak. Facts are poorly organized. **Voice:** The writer often did not paraphrase. **Word Choice:** Language is inexact. **Sentence Fluency:** The report shows little sentence variety. **Conventions:** There may be many mistakes. **Presentation:** The final copy may be somewhat difficult to read.

2

Ideas: The report lacks focus and details. The bibliography is incomplete or missing. **Organization:** Facts are unorganized. The report ends abruptly. **Voice:** The writer rarely paraphrases. **Word Choice:** Language is unclear. **Sentence Fluency:** Sentences lack variety. **Conventions:** Mistakes sometimes make the report confusing. **Presentation:** The final copy may be messy.

1

Ideas: The report lacks focus and details. The bibliography is missing. **Organization:** Information is disorganized or just listed. **Voice:** The writer copied the text from sources. **Word Choice:** Words are inexact or repetitive. **Sentence Fluency:** Sentences are very short, unclear, or repetitive. **Conventions:** Many mistakes make the paper hard to understand. **Presentation:** The final copy is messy and often illegible.

6

Ideas: The story focuses on an interesting problem and characters that are brought to life with colorful details and lively dialogue. **Organization:** The story has a strong beginning, middle, and end. Events are in a clear order. **Voice:** A strong voice enlivens the story. **Word Choice:** Many exact, descriptive words create a vivid picture. **Sentence Fluency:** Sentences exhibit interesting variety and flow smoothly. **Conventions:** There are few, if any, errors. **Presentation:** The final copy is neat and legible.

5

Ideas: The story focuses on a clear problem and characters that are developed with details and dialogue. **Organization:** The story has a clear beginning, middle, and end. Events are generally told in order. **Voice:** The writing catches the reader's attention. **Word Choice:** Exact words create a clear picture. **Sentence Fluency:** Sentences sound natural, and there is good variety. **Conventions:** There are few errors. **Presentation:** The final copy is generally neat and legible.

4

Ideas: The plot may not focus on a clear problem, and some events may be unimportant. More details and dialogue are needed to develop the characters. **Organization:** The story has a beginning, middle, and end, but they may not be equally interesting. **Voice:** The writing could be more interesting. **Word Choice:** The story needs more exact words. **Sentence Fluency:** The story needs greater sentence variety. **Conventions:** Mistakes do not affect understanding. **Presentation:** The final copy may be a bit messy but is legible.

3

Ideas: The plot may not focus on a clear problem, and some events may be unimportant. Many more details and dialogue are needed to develop the characters. **Organization:** Parts of the story are confusing or undeveloped. **Voice:** The writing is often uninteresting. **Word Choice:** The writer uses few exact words. **Sentence Fluency:** The story shows little sentence variety. **Conventions:** There may be a number of mistakes. **Presentation:** The final copy may be somewhat difficult to read.

2

Ideas: The plot lacks a clear problem, or it is undeveloped. Parts of the story may be missing or unfocused. There is little detail or dialogue. **Organization:** The story is disorganized or confusing. **Voice:** The writing rarely holds the reader's interest. **Word Choice:** Word choice is repetitive or inexact. **Sentence Fluency:** The story lacks sentence variety. **Conventions:** Mistakes sometimes make the story hard to understand. **Presentation:** The final copy may be messy and hard to read.

1

Ideas: The paper may only be a series of events with no plot. There are no details. It is difficult to understand. **Organization:** The story lacks a clear beginning, middle, and end and is confusing. **Voice:** The writing is dull and flat. **Word Choice:** Word choice is vague and uninteresting. **Sentence Fluency:** Sentences are short, unclear, or repetitive. **Conventions:** Many mistakes make the paper hard to understand. **Presentation:** The final copy is messy and often illegible.

Grades 5–6 Writing Traits Scoring Rubric: Description

6

Ideas: The description focuses on one topic, using many vivid, interesting details. **Organization:** Details are well organized. An interesting beginning introduces the topic. A good ending wraps up the description. **Voice:** The writer's voice is strong. **Word Choice:** Many exact, sensory words create a vivid picture. **Sentence Fluency:** Sentences exhibit interesting variety and flow smoothly. **Conventions:** There are few, if any, errors. **Presentation:** The final copy is neat and legible.

5

Ideas: The writer uses vivid details to describe a clear topic. **Organization:** Details are generally well organized. The beginning introduces the topic. The ending wraps up the description. **Voice:** The writer's voice is evident. **Word Choice:** Exact, sensory words create a clear picture, but more would be beneficial. **Sentence Fluency:** Sentences sound natural, and there is good variety. **Conventions:** There are few errors. **Presentation:** The final copy is generally neat and legible.

4

Ideas: The description focuses on a topic, but more vivid details are needed. **Organization:** The organization is generally clear. The beginning and the ending may be somewhat weak. **Voice:** The writer's voice could be stronger. **Word Choice:** The writer could have used more exact words and more sensory words. **Sentence Fluency:** The paper needs greater sentence variety. **Conventions:** Mistakes do not affect understanding. **Presentation:** The final copy may be a bit messy but is legible.

3

Ideas: The description focuses on a topic but may contain extraneous details. Many more details are needed. **Organization:** Details are somewhat organized. The beginning and the ending may be weak. **Voice:** The writer's voice is weak. **Word Choice:** The paper needs many more exact, sensory words. **Sentence Fluency:** The paper shows little sentence variety. **Conventions:** There may be a number of mistakes. **Presentation:** The final copy may be somewhat difficult to read.

2

Ideas: The description may not be clearly focused on a topic. Few details are included. **Organization:** Details are not organized. The beginning and ending are weak or missing. **Voice:** The writer's voice is weak or missing. **Word Choice:** The writer uses few exact words or sensory words. **Sentence Fluency:** The paper lacks sentence variety. **Conventions:** Mistakes sometimes make the paper hard to understand. **Presentation:** The final copy may be messy and hard to read.

1

Ideas: The description may not be focused. There are no details, or they are inappropriate. **Organization:** Details are disorganized. The beginning and ending are missing. **Voice:** The paper lacks voice. **Word Choice:** Word choice is vague or uninteresting. It may be confusing. **Sentence Fluency:** Sentences are very short, unclear, or repetitive. **Conventions:** Many mistakes make the paper hard to understand. **Presentation:** The final copy is messy. It may be illegible in many places.

6

Ideas: The essay supports an opinion with strong reasons and clear, exact details. **Organization:** Reasons and details are in well-organized paragraphs. An interesting introduction states the opinion; the conclusion summarizes it. **Voice:** The writer's voice is strong. **Word Choice:** Words are precise, active, and descriptive. **Sentence Fluency:** Sentences exhibit interesting variety and flow smoothly. **Conventions:** There are few, if any, errors. **Presentation:** The final copy is neat and legible.

5

Ideas: The essay supports an opinion with good reasons and details, but more details would be helpful. **Organization:** Reasons and details are organized in paragraphs. The introduction and conclusion are appropriate. **Voice:** The writer's voice is evident. **Word Choice:** Language is interesting and exact, but additional exact words are needed. **Sentence Fluency:** Sentences sound natural, and there is good variety. **Conventions:** There are few errors. **Presentation:** The final copy is generally neat and legible.

4

Ideas: Several reasons support an opinion, but one reason may be weak. More details are needed. **Organization:** The introduction or conclusion may be weak. Some parts could be better developed or organized. **Voice:** The writer's voice could be stronger. **Word Choice:** More exact, interesting words are needed. **Sentence Fluency:** The essay needs greater sentence variety. **Conventions:** Mistakes do not affect understanding. **Presentation:** The final copy may be a bit messy but is legible.

3

Ideas: The essay focuses on an opinion, but it needs more or stronger reasons. Many additional details are needed. **Organization:** The introduction or conclusion may be weak. Many parts are not well developed or organized. **Voice:** The writer's voice may be weak. **Word Choice:** Language is inexact or boring. **Sentence Fluency:** The essay shows little sentence variety. **Conventions:** There may be many mistakes. **Presentation:** The final copy may be somewhat difficult to read.

2

Ideas: The essay sometimes loses focus. Reasons and details are weak. **Organization:** The introduction or conclusion may be missing. Ideas are poorly organized. **Voice:** The writer's voice may be missing or weak. **Word Choice:** Word choice is limited and repetitive. **Sentence Fluency:** The essay lacks sentence variety. **Conventions:** Mistakes sometimes make the essay hard to understand. **Presentation:** The final copy may be messy and hard to read.

1

Ideas: The essay may not focus on an opinion, or it may express several opinions with little support. **Organization:** The paper may be just a list of thoughts or written as one paragraph. **Voice:** There is no voice. The writing sounds flat. **Word Choice:** Word choice is vague or uninteresting. It may be confusing. **Sentence Fluency:** Sentences are very short, unclear, or repetitive. **Conventions:** Many mistakes make the essay hard to understand. **Presentation:** The final copy is messy and often illegible.

Grades 5–6 Writing Traits Scoring Rubric: Personal Narrative

6

Ideas: The narrative focuses on a single experience. Many well-chosen details tell what the writer saw, heard, tasted, smelled, and felt. **Organization:** The beginning and ending are strong. Events are told in a clear order. **Voice:** The writer expresses his or her personality. **Word Choice:** The writer uses numerous exact, interesting words. **Sentence Fluency:** Sentences exhibit interesting variety and flow smoothly. **Conventions:** There are few, if any, errors. **Presentation:** The final copy is neat and legible.

5

Ideas: The narrative focuses on a single experience. Details tell what the writer saw, heard, tasted, smelled, and felt. **Organization:** The beginning is good. The narrative is generally well organized. **Voice:** The writer's personality is evident. **Word Choice:** The writer uses exact, interesting words, although more would be desirable. **Sentence Fluency:** Sentences sound natural, and there is good variety. **Conventions:** There are few errors. **Presentation:** The final copy is generally neat and legible.

4

Ideas: The narrative generally focuses on one experience, but it may include extraneous information. More details are needed. **Organization:** The beginning or ending could be stronger. The order of events may be unclear. **Voice:** The writer's voice could be stronger. **Word Choice:** Additional exact words are needed. **Sentence Fluency:** The paper needs greater sentence variety. **Conventions:** Mistakes do not affect understanding. **Presentation:** The final copy may be a bit messy but is legible.

3

Ideas: The narrative has a clear topic but includes extraneous information. Many additional details are needed. **Organization:** The beginning or ending may be weak or missing. The order of events may be unclear. **Voice:** The writer's voice is somewhat weak. **Word Choice:** Word choice may be repetitive or inexact. **Sentence Fluency:** The paper shows little sentence variety. **Conventions:** There may be a number of mistakes. **Presentation:** The final copy may be somewhat difficult to read.

2

Ideas: The narrative has a topic, but it lacks details or includes much extraneous information. **Organization:** The beginning or ending is dull or missing. The order of events is confusing. **Voice:** The writer's voice is missing or weak. **Word Choice:** Word choice is limited and repetitive. **Sentence Fluency:** The paper lacks sentence variety. **Conventions:** Mistakes sometimes make the paper hard to understand. **Presentation:** The final copy may be messy and hard to read.

1

Ideas: The narrative does not focus on one experience. There are few or no details. It is hard to understand what happened. **Organization:** There may be no clear beginning, middle, or end. **Voice:** The writer's voice is bored or missing. **Word Choice:** Word choice is vague, repetitive, or confusing. **Sentence Fluency:** Sentences are very short, unclear, or repetitive. **Conventions:** Many mistakes make the paper hard to understand. **Presentation:** The final copy is messy and often illegible.

6

Ideas: The essay focuses on a clear goal supported by at least three convincing reasons and strong facts and details. **Organization:** An interesting beginning states the goal. Support is presented in well-developed paragraphs. **Voice:** The writer clearly expresses feelings. **Word Choice:** The writer uses effective persuasive language. **Sentence Fluency:** Sentences exhibit interesting variety and flow smoothly. **Conventions:** There are few, if any, errors. **Presentation:** The final copy is neat and legible.

5

Ideas: The essay focuses on a goal supported by strong reasons, facts, and details, although more support may be needed. **Organization:** The beginning states the goal. Reasons and supporting facts and details are organized into logical paragraphs. **Voice:** The writer expresses feelings. **Word Choice:** The writer uses persuasive language. **Sentence Fluency:** Sentences sound natural, and there is good variety. **Conventions:** There are few errors. **Presentation:** The final copy is generally neat and legible.

4

Ideas: The essay focuses on a goal with supporting reasons, facts, and details. More support is needed. **Organization:** A few facts and details may be misplaced. The beginning may be boring. **Voice:** The writer could express more feelings about the goal. **Word Choice:** The essay needs more persuasive language. **Sentence Fluency:** The essay needs greater sentence variety. **Conventions:** Mistakes do not affect understanding. **Presentation:** The final copy may be a bit messy but is legible.

3

Ideas: The essay mostly focuses on a goal with supporting reasons, facts, and examples. The goal may be unclear, and the support may be weak. **Organization:** Supporting information may not be clearly organized. **Voice:** The writer's feelings may be unclear or vague. **Word Choice:** The essay has little persuasive language. **Sentence Fluency:** The essay shows little sentence variety. **Conventions:** There may be many mistakes. **Presentation:** The final copy may be somewhat difficult to read.

2

Ideas: The essay does not focus on a goal, or support is limited and unconvincing. **Organization:** The goal is not stated. Support is poorly organized. **Voice:** The writer does not express feelings about the goal. **Word Choice:** Language is boring and unpersuasive. **Sentence Fluency:** The essay lacks sentence variety. **Conventions:** Mistakes sometimes make the essay hard to understand. **Presentation:** The final copy may be messy and hard to read.

1

Ideas: The goal is unclear. There is no support, or it is unconvincing. **Organization:** Ideas are unorganized or just listed. **Voice:** The voice is missing. **Word Choice:** Language is vague and unpersuasive. **Sentence Fluency:** Sentences are very short, unclear, or repetitive. **Conventions:** Many mistakes make the essay hard to understand. **Presentation:** The final copy is messy and often illegible.

Grades 5–6 Writing Traits Scoring Rubric: Research Report

6

Ideas: The paper is a well-researched, factual report about a clear topic with a complete, accurate bibliography. **Organization:** Information is well organized into paragraphs with strong topic sentences, supporting facts and examples, and an effective beginning and conclusion. **Voice:** The writer uses his or her own words. **Word Choice:** Words are precise, active, and descriptive. **Sentence Fluency:** Sentences exhibit good variety and flow smoothly. **Conventions:** There are few, if any, errors. **Presentation:** The final copy is neat and legible.

5

Ideas: The paper presents researched facts about a clear topic. It has a good bibliography. **Organization:** Facts are grouped into paragraphs with topic sentences. It includes a good beginning and conclusion. **Voice:** The writer uses his or her own words. **Word Choice:** Words are exact. **Sentence Fluency:** Sentences sound natural. There is good variety. **Conventions:** There are few errors. **Presentation:** The final copy is generally neat and legible.

4

Ideas: More facts are needed. The bibliography may be incomplete. **Organization:** More topic sentences are needed. Facts may not be well organized. The conclusion may be weak. **Voice:** The writer mostly uses his or her own words. **Word Choice:** More exact words are needed. **Sentence Fluency:** The report needs more sentence variety. **Conventions:** Mistakes do not affect understanding. **Presentation:** The final copy may be a bit messy but is legible.

3

Ideas: The paper is not clearly focused. More facts are needed. The bibliography may be incomplete. **Organization:** Topic sentences are missing or weak. Facts are poorly organized. **Voice:** The writer often did not paraphrase. **Word Choice:** Language is inexact. **Sentence Fluency:** The report shows little sentence variety. **Conventions:** There may be many mistakes. **Presentation:** The final copy may be somewhat difficult to read.

2

Ideas: The report lacks focus and details. The bibliography is incomplete or missing. **Organization:** Facts are unorganized. The report ends abruptly. **Voice:** The writer rarely paraphrases. **Word Choice:** Language is inexact. **Sentence Fluency:** Sentences lack variety. **Conventions:** Mistakes sometimes make the report hard to understand. **Presentation:** The final copy may be messy.

1

Ideas: The report lacks focus and details. The bibliography is missing or inaccurate. **Organization:** Information is disorganized, unclear, or just listed. **Voice:** The writer copied text from sources. **Word Choice:** Words may be vague, uninteresting, or confusing. **Sentence Fluency:** Sentences are very short, unclear, or repetitive. **Conventions:** Many mistakes make the paper hard to understand. **Presentation:** The final copy is messy and often illegible.

6

Ideas: The story focuses on an interesting, well-developed plot and characters brought to life through colorful details and lively dialogue. **Organization:** The story has a strong beginning, middle, and end. Events are told in a clear order. **Voice:** The writing captivates and creates the mood. **Word Choice:** Many exact words create a vivid picture. **Sentence Fluency:** Sentences exhibit interesting variety and flow smoothly. **Conventions:** There are few, if any, errors. **Presentation:** The final copy is neat and legible.

5

Ideas: The story focuses on a clear problem and characters that are developed with details and dialogue. **Organization:** The story has a clear beginning, middle, and end. Events are generally told in order. **Voice:** The writing holds the reader's interest and creates a mood. **Word Choice:** Exact words create a clear picture. **Sentence Fluency:** Sentences sound natural, and there is good variety. **Conventions:** There are few errors. **Presentation:** The final copy is generally neat and legible.

4

Ideas: The plot may not focus on a clear problem. Some events may be unimportant. More details and dialogue are needed. **Organization:** The beginning, middle, or ending could be stronger. **Voice:** The writing may not hold the reader's interest or create a mood. **Word Choice:** The story needs more exact words. **Sentence Fluency:** The story needs greater sentence variety. **Conventions:** Mistakes do not affect understanding. **Presentation:** The final copy may be a bit messy but is legible.

3

Ideas: The plot may not clearly focus on a problem, and some events may be unimportant. Many more details and dialogue are needed. **Organization:** Parts of the story are confusing or undeveloped. **Voice:** The writing is often uninteresting and does not create a mood. **Word Choice:** The writer uses few exact words. **Sentence Fluency:** The story shows little sentence variety. **Conventions:** There may be a number of mistakes. **Presentation:** The final copy may be somewhat difficult to read.

2

Ideas: The plot lacks a clear problem, or it is undeveloped. Parts of the story may be missing or include unimportant information. There is little detail or dialogue. **Organization:** The story is disorganized or confusing. **Voice:** The writing rarely holds the reader's interest. **Word Choice:** Word choice is repetitive or inexact. **Sentence Fluency:** The story lacks sentence variety. **Conventions:** Mistakes sometimes make the story hard to understand. **Presentation:** The final copy may be messy and hard to read.

1

Ideas: The paper may only be a series of events with no plot. There are no details. It is difficult to understand. **Organization:** The story lacks a clear beginning, middle, and end and is confusing. **Voice:** The writing is dull and flat. **Word Choice:** Word choice is vague and uninteresting. **Sentence Fluency:** Sentences are very short, unclear, or repetitive. **Conventions:** Many mistakes make the paper hard to understand. **Presentation:** The final copy is messy and often illegible.

HOUGHTON MIFFLIN READING provides many opportunities for students to improve in the various writing traits.

- Writing Skills Lessons
- Writing Traits
- Responding activities
- Journal Writing
- Grammar Skills Lessons
- Daily Language Practice
- Grammar Reteaching Lessons
- Resources for Writing

In addition, each theme's Reading-Writing Workshop helps students use the traits in writing a complete paper of a specific type. You can emphasize specific traits at the various steps of the writing process, as shown in the graphic below.

Writing Traits in the Writing Process

Analytic Scoring

Analytic scoring assesses individual elements of a piece of writing by describing them according to specific criteria and assigning them numerical values on a rubric. These elements, or traits, may include content and purpose, organization, fluency, word choice, voice, conventions, and presentation.

Because analytic scoring rubrics rate specific traits, they are useful for diagnosing as well as assessing the strengths and weaknesses of students' writing. Analytic scoring rubrics

- show students and teachers in which ways the writing is strong and in which it needs improvement;
- allow teachers to provide students with a great deal of information clearly and consistently;
- help teachers identify the accomplishments and needs of both individual students and the class as a group; and
- help a school or a district identify instructional objectives, structure an appropriate curriculum, and assess results.

There are two types of analytic scoring rubrics: general rubrics and mode-specific rubrics. The General Analytic Writing Traits Scoring Rubric on page 61 can be used to evaluate most types of writing. It uses a numerical scale, as a holistic scoring rubric does, but the scores apply to separate traits rather than to an entire piece of writing. Instead of giving the paper an overall score of 4, you might score content as a 5, organization as a 3, and so on. The rubric uses a five-point scale, which allows you easily to weight individual traits (see page 62) and to convert scores to percents for assigning letter grades. You can use the General Analytic Writing Traits Scoring Sheet on page 112 to evaluate single pieces of writing for students.

The criteria for each trait, or category, on the General Analytic Writing Traits Scoring Rubric have been developed from rubrics used in various states. Of course, you will need to interpret the criteria appropriately for your grade level: a score of 4 in content at Grade 1, for example, is not the same as a 4 at Grade 5.

GENERAL ANALYTIC WRITING TRAITS SCORING RUBRIC

Trait	5	3	1
Ideas and Content	• The ideas are clear, fresh, and/or original. • The writing is focused. • The main ideas support the topic. • The details support the main ideas.	• The ideas are somewhat unclear or trite. • The focus needs to be clearer. • The writing doesn't always hold the reader's attention. • There are too few details or they are irrelevant.	• The ideas are unclear. • The purpose is unclear or incorrectly focused. • The writing repeats information or presents information as a list rather than in paragraphs. • There is no elaboration.
Organization	• The beginning is engaging. • The writing is well organized. • Main ideas and supporting details are logically grouped. • Transitional words are used. • The conclusion is strong.	• The beginning is somewhat weak. • The writing needs a clearer organization. • The arrangement of main ideas and details is disjointed. • The conclusion is weak.	• There is no real beginning to the paper. • The writing lacks organization and is confusing. • The ideas aren't connected. • There is no conclusion.
Voice	• The writer's personality can be heard. • The writer conveys his or her feelings. • The reader feels connected to the writer and gets a sense of humor, suspense, etc., from the writing.	• A sense of the writer's personality is conveyed somewhat weakly. • The writer doesn't express his or her feelings well. • The reader sometimes feels connected to the writer.	• The writer's personality cannot be heard. • The writing lacks any feeling or emotion. • The reader does not feel connected to the writer.
Word Choice	• The words chosen are precise, active, and descriptive, and they convey a clear mental picture. • Word choice is appropriate to the purpose and the audience.	• Word choice could be more interesting and precise. • Some words may be used incorrectly. • Word choice may be somewhat inappropriate to the purpose and the audience.	• Word choice lacks interest and precision. • Many words are used incorrectly. • Word choice is inappropriate to the purpose and the audience.
Sentence Fluency	• The writing flows smoothly and sounds natural. • Sentence length and structure are varied.	• The writing moves along but may sound repetitive and stilted. • More sentence variety is needed.	• The writing is mechanical or unwieldy. • There is no sentence variety.
Conventions	• The writing follows standard capitalization, punctuation, spelling, and usage rules. • Any mistakes do not detract.	• There are some errors in capitalization, punctuation, spelling, and usage. • Mistakes cause some confusion.	• There are many errors in spelling, capitalization, usage, and punctuation. • Mistakes affect understanding.
Presentation	• The paper is ⬛⬛⬛ the handwriting ⬛⬛⬛ legible. • The writing fol⬛⬛⬛orrect format.	• The writing is legible but is somewhat difficult to read. • The writing generally follows the correct format.	• The writing is barely legible. • Correct format is not used.

The General Analytic Writing Traits Scoring Rubric can also be adapted for specific writing types. For example, for persuasive writing, the Score 5 criteria for *Ideas and Content* might be these:

- The writer's goal is clearly stated.
- The writing is focused.
- The reasons support the goal.
- Facts and examples support the reasons.

You can also delete traits that you are not stressing in a certain assignment.

To use a general or a mode-specific analytic rubric, read the paper carefully; then skim it and assign a score for each trait.

- Depending on your experience and preference, you may choose to skim separately for each trait.
- What you are teaching may influence the importance you assign to certain traits. Therefore, you may not feel that you have to read every paper for every trait every time.
- At times, you may want to alter your expectations. For example, as students try new writing types or work on specific writing traits, you can encourage them to learn and experiment by not expecting mastery at the beginning.

CONVERTING ANALYTIC SCORES

Since an analytic scale allows more precise evaluation of a composition, you may not want to give all elements equal weight. Many teachers, for example, give less weight to conventions and presentation than they do to content and organization. The conversion table below shows a typical range of weights and allows for reporting scores on a 100-point scale.

Trait	Score	Weight of Trait	Total Trait Score
Ideas and Content	____ of a possible 5	x 4	____ of a possible 20
Organization	____ of a possible 5	x 4	____ of a possible 20
Voice	____ of a possible 5	x 3	____ of a possible 15
Word Choice	____ of a possible 5	x 3	____ of a possible 15
Sentence Fluency	____ of a possible 5	x 3	____ of a possible 15
Conventions	____ of a possible 5	x 2	____ of a possible 10
Presentation	____ of a possible 5	x 1	____ of a possible 5
Score for Paper on 100-Point Scale			____ of a possible 100

USING ANALYTIC SCORING RESULTS TO PLAN INSTRUCTION

The array of a student's scores on a paper or group of papers can give you valuable insight into the student's instructional needs. Your greatest concern should be traits scoring in the 1–2 range. The chart below shows Tarika's scores for three pieces of writing. Because the description and the response piece were done in less time and with less supervision than the workshop piece, you might conclude that Tarika's fluency and use of conventions improve when she is given time and encouragement to revise.

Name: Tarika	Content	Organization	Voice	Word Choice	Fluency	Conventions	Presentation
Description, 1/12	4	3	4	3	②	②	3
Response piece, 1/14	3	3	3	3	②	①	②
Workshop: Persuasive Essay, 1/15–1/17	4	3	4	3	3	3	4

You can also arrange class scores for a particular assignment on the same grid. The pattern of high and low scores will tell you where to concentrate your instruction and can help you group students for reteaching activities. An Analytic Writing Traits Scoring Overview Grid appears on page 113 in this handbook.

Assignment: Reading-Writing Workshop Persuasive Essay, 1/15–1/17	Content	Organization	Voice	Word Choice	Fluency	Conventions	Presentation
Tarika	4	3	4	3	3	3	4
Becky	3	②	3	②	②	①	②
Kevin	②	②	4	3	①	②	3
Ariel	4	3	4	②	3	②	3
Akira	3	②	3	3	3	3	3
Luis	3	3	②	3	3	3	4

Part 7

Formal Assessment of Progress

Introduction

Formal assessment occurs anytime teachers suspend instruction to assess their students. Formal assessments include teacher-made tests, tests that accompany published programs, and state- or district-mandated standardized tests.

In the past, teachers often used formal assessment as the sole measure of a student's success. But formal assessment is just one part of the picture in an assessment-based literacy classroom. In addition, students' test scores, like their classroom performance, depend on many factors and can vary from day to day. Therefore, it is essential that teachers weigh test scores against daily observations of students, anecdotal records, homework assignments, and the portfolios of work compiled to show progress throughout the year. This balanced approach to assessment gives teachers the best insights into their students' skills, abilities, knowledge, and academic growth.

The Tests in HOUGHTON MIFFLIN READING

Many teachers want options when it comes to formal assessment, so HOUGHTON MIFFLIN READING offers three types of tests: *Integrated Theme Tests, Theme Skills Tests,* and *Benchmark Progress Tests.* Each of these tests is meant to be used in conjunction with ongoing informal assessment to measure your students' progress and to help you plan instruction.

Each test has a different purpose. Choose the tests, or a combination of them, that best meet your needs. To determine which of the three tests, or what combination of tests, you want to use in your classroom, think about

- your own curriculum goals, as well as those of your district and state;
- your formal assessment goals;
- your testing preferences and scheduling limitations; and
- the type of information you want about your students.

INTEGRATED THEME TESTS

The *Integrated Theme Tests* (Grades K–6) allow students to apply learned skills and strategies to new theme-related text selections. Each test, given after students have completed the corresponding theme, has four parts, as follows:

- **Grade K** comprehension, phonemic awareness, phonics, writing;

- **Grade 1** reading strategy, comprehension, phonics, writing and language;

- **Grade 2** reading strategy, comprehension/comparing texts, phonics and vocabulary, writing and language;

- **Grades 3–6** reading strategy, comprehension/comparing texts, structural analysis and vocabulary, writing and language.

Each of the *Integrated Theme Tests* has these features:

- both multiple-choice and open-response comprehension questions (with a scoring rubric in the Teacher's Annotated Edition);

- theme-related writing prompts (with a scoring rubric and anchor papers in the Teacher's Annotated Edition);

- suggestions for three levels of extra support to meet individual needs among students taking the regular tests;

- alternative-format tests for use with struggling older readers or students with special needs;

- an optional listening-comprehension section;

- an optional student self-assessment survey.

Each test can be completed in about an hour or in two thirty-minute sittings on successive days. For more information on using the results of the *Integrated Theme Tests* to plan for instruction, see page T8 in the test booklet. The blackline master on page 115 of this handbook is a Class Record sheet that will allow you to view your class's scores on the test for grouping purposes.

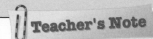

Teacher's Note

Because the *Integrated Theme Tests* are short, applying a strict grading percentage is not appropriate. The points noted in parentheses (90–100 for Excellent, for example) are score ranges. If you need to translate these scores into letter grades, you can use the following:

A Excellent (90–100)
B Good (75–89)
C Some progress (60–74)
D Needs improvement (0–59)

Home/Community Connection

Sending Test Scores to Parents
You might want to photocopy the Self-Assessment page from students' *Integrated Theme Tests* to send to parents. Include on the same page your own note giving the student's score and inviting parents to come in and look at the test itself if they wish.

THEME SKILLS TESTS

The *Theme Skills Tests* (Grades K–6) assess specific reading and language skills taught in each theme of HOUGHTON MIFFLIN READING. Separate test sections, or subtests, in multiple-choice format cover each of these skills:

- **Grade K** phonemic awareness, comprehension, phonics, high-frequency words;

- **Grade 1** phonics/decoding, high-frequency words, comprehension skills, spelling (Themes 3–10), grammar (Themes 3–10), writing skills (Themes 5–10);

- **Grade 2** phonics/decoding, high-frequency words, comprehension skills, information and study skills, spelling, vocabulary, grammar, writing skills;

- **Grades 3–6** comprehension skills, information and study skills, structural analysis, spelling, vocabulary, grammar, writing skills.

You can use the *Theme Skills Tests* in a variety of ways.

- Give them as pretests or as posttests.

- Give some students individual subtests to supplement the *Integrated Theme Tests* when you need more information.

- Give individual subtests throughout the year, as pretests to help you plan instructional support and as posttests to assess specific reading and language skills or your reteaching efforts.

- Let students use them as practice for standardized multiple-choice tests.

The Class Record blackline master on page 116 of this handbook will allow you to view your class's scores for grouping purposes.

BENCHMARK PROGRESS TESTS

The *Benchmark Progress Tests* (Grades 1–6) are holistic, comprehensive measures of your students' reading and writing achievement. They permit you to compare your students' performance with that of other students at the same grade level nationwide. You can give *Benchmark Progress Tests* anytime during the school year to find a student's reading level, or you can give the test at the beginning, middle, and end of the school year to assess overall progress. Each test includes

- a Practice Test that can be used to help familiarize students with the test format and reduce students' test anxiety;

- both a narrative and an expository selection;

- a variety of test formats, including multiple-choice questions, short-answer questions, writing prompts, and self-assessment questions;

- in the Teacher's Annotated Edition, scoring rubrics and sample answers for short-answer questions, and scoring rubrics and anchor papers for each writing prompt.

Modifying Instruction Based on Formal Assessment of Progress

The following chart outlines and organizes by skill the formal assessment measures discussed in Part 7. It also lists the resources in HOUGHTON MIFFLIN READING that you can use to provide extra support for and to challenge students.

TE: Teacher's Edition   **TRB:** Teacher's Resource Blackline Masters   **PB:** Practice Book   **BLMs:** Blackline Masters   **Parenthetical numbers:** grade levels

If you want to assess...	You can use...	Then you can...	
		give extra support	challenge
Phonemic Awareness and Phonics/Decoding	Integrated Theme Tests Theme Skills Test	TE: Phonemic Awareness activities in Opening Routines **(K–1)** and in the Phonics section **(K–2)**; Extra Support/Intervention boxes, Monitoring Student Progress in Phonics lessons **(K–2)**; Phonics Center activities **(K–1)**; Listening Center: Alphafriend Audios, Alphafolders **(K)** TE, Resources: Reteaching Lessons for Phonics **(1–2)** Other Reading: Phonics Library BLMs, On My Way Practice Readers **(K–2)** *Extra Support Handbook* **(K–2)** CD-ROMs: *Lexia Phonics Primary Intervention* **(K–2)**; *Get Set for Reading* **(1–6)**; *Curious George Learns Phonics* **(K–2)**	Other Reading: Little Big Books **(K–1)**; Classroom Bookshelf **(K–6)**
Structural Analysis/Phonics	Integrated Theme Tests Theme Skills Tests	TE, Resources: Reteaching Lessons for Structural Analysis Skills **(3–6)**	TE, Resources: Challenge/Extension Activities for Phonics **(1–2)**

If you want to assess...	You can use...	Then you can...	
		give extra support	**challenge**
Structural Analysis/Phonics (continued)		Other Reading: Leveled Readers Theme Paperbacks (easy), Classroom Bookshelf (easy) **(K–6)** *Extra Support Handbook* **(3–6)** CD-ROMs: *Get Set for Reading* **(1–6)**; *Lexia Phonics Intermediate Intervention* **(3–6)**	Other Reading: Theme Paperbacks (above level) **(1–2)**, Classroom Bookshelf **(K–6)** CD-ROM: *Wacky Web Tales* **(3–6)**
High-Frequency Words	Theme Skills Tests	TE: Monitoring Student Progress, High-Frequency Word Practice in Word Work sections **(K–2)** TE, Resources: Reteaching Lessons for High-Frequency Words **(1–2)** Other Reading: On My Way Practice Readers **(K–2)**; Phonics Library BLMs **(K–2)** *Extra Support Handbook* **(K–2)**	TE, Resources: Challenge/Extension Activities for High-Frequency Words **(1–2)** Other Reading: Little Big Books **(K–1)**, Classroom Bookshelf **(K–6)**
Reading Strategies	Integrated Theme Tests	TE, each selection: Extra Support/ Intervention boxes **(1–6)** TE: Strategy Focus **(K–6)**; Strategy Review, Strategy/Skill Preview, Extra Support/Intervention Strategy Modeling **(2–6)** TE, Big Books: Strategy Preview/Focus **(K–1)** PB: Strategy Poster **(1–6)** *Extra Support Handbook* (Phonics/Decoding Strategy) **(K–6)**	TE, each selection: Challenge boxes **(1–6)** Other Reading: Theme Paperbacks (above level), Classroom Bookshelf (above level) **(K–6)**
Comprehension/ Comparing Texts	Integrated Theme Tests Theme Skills Tests Benchmark Progress Tests	TE: Retelling or Summarizing prompts in Responding section **(K)**; Building Background **(K–6)**; Key Concepts **(K–3)** TE, each selection: Extra Support/Intervention boxes; Writing Support for Responding; Previewing the Text boxes **(1–6)**; Revisiting the Selection boxes **(K–6)**; Comprehension Review lessons **(2–6)**	TE: Center Activities in Responding section **(K)** TE, each selection: Challenge boxes **(K–6)** and Assignment Cards **(2–6)**; Responding questions and activities **(K–2)** TE, Theme Resources: Challenge/Extension Activities for Comprehension **(1–6)**

If you want to assess...	You can use...	Then you can...	
		give extra support	challenge
Comprehension/ Comparing Texts (continued)		TE, Resources: Reteaching Lessons for Comprehension Skills (1–6) TRB: Selection Summaries (2–6) Other Reading: On My Way Practice Readers, Phonics Library BLMs (K–2); Leveled Readers Theme Paperbacks (below level) (1–6); Classroom Bookshelf (below level) (K–6) *Extra Support Handbook* (1–6) CD-ROM: *Get Set for Reading* (1–6) Anthology Audios (1–6)	Other Reading: Little Big Books (K–2), Theme Paperbacks (above level) (1–6); Classroom Bookshelf (above level) (K–6) *Challenge Handbook* (K–6)
Listening Comprehension	Integrated Theme Tests	TE: Teacher Read Aloud, Listening/Speaking/Viewing (2–6)	TE: Listening/Speaking/ Viewing (2–6) *Challenge Handbook* (K–6)
Spelling	Theme Skills Tests	TE, Spelling: Basic Words, Extra Support/Intervention boxes (1–6) CD-ROM: *Curious George Learns to Spell* (1–2)	TE, Spelling: Challenge Words (1–6); Challenge boxes (1–6)
Vocabulary	Integrated Theme Tests Theme Skills Tests	TE, each selection: Developing Key Vocabulary, Vocabulary boxes (2–6)	TE, Vocabulary Skills: Expanding Your Vocabulary (2–6) TE, Resources: Challenge/Extension Activities for Vocabulary (2–6) *Challenge Handbook* (K–6) CD-ROM: *Wacky Web Tales* (3–6)
Writing	Integrated Theme Tests Benchmark Progress Tests	TE: Shared, Interactive, Independent writing lessons (K) TE, Reading-Writing Workshop: Student Writing Model, Writing Traits notes, Student Self-Assessment (1–6)	TE, each selection: Journal Writing, Genre Lessons, Writer's Craft Lessons (1–6) TE, Reading-Writing Workshop: Reading as a Writer, Publishing and Evaluating (1–6) TE, Resources: Writing Activities (2–6) *Challenge Handbook* (K–6)
Grammar	Theme Skills Tests	TE: Grammar Review Lessons (1) TE, Resources: Reteaching Lessons for Grammar Skills (2–6) *Extra Support Handbook* (3–6)	CD-ROM: *Wacky Web Tales* (3–6)

Part 8

Preparing Students for Standardized Tests

Introduction

Standardized tests are designed to give a common, or "standard," measure of students' performance. Traditionally, states or districts have used standardized test results to make decisions about student promotion, placement, or graduation, as well as about curriculum and instruction. These tests have also been used to evaluate the effectiveness of schools.

In many states, standardized tests have taken on increased importance in recent years. They are the subject of much controversy as well as the cause of anxiety for some students. It is important, therefore, to help your students learn *how* to take standardized tests. It is also important for you as a teacher to understand the purposes, uses, and limitations of these tests.

In your effort to help your students learn how to take tests, remember that teaching test-taking strategies is not the same as "teaching to the test." Focusing on teaching only the skills that will be tested limits the breadth of your curriculum and can lead to teaching skills in isolation rather than in the context of authentic literacy activities.

The literacy instruction you are giving your students now—to prepare them for continued schooling and their lives ahead—will also give them the skills necessary to perform on standardized tests. Nevertheless, you can help your students even more by teaching them specific *strategies* to use in taking these tests.

Strategies

Test-taking strategies are a set of skills that your students can apply in varied testing situations. Often, a student who has demonstrated an understanding and ability to apply a skill in your classroom may be unable to apply this same skill on a formal test because of problems such as

- unfamiliarity with the test's procedures or format;

- distractions surrounding the test or the testing environment;

- fear of the test's time restrictions;

- stress and anxiety.

Knowing some simple test-taking strategies will help students overcome many of these problems. On page 117 you will find a Test-Taking Strategies blackline master to distribute to your class. Reviewing these strategies each time they take a standardized test will help students memorize the strategies and be able to use them almost instinctively.

TESTING PROCEDURES

You can work with students in several ways to familiarize them with the forms and procedures typically used in standardized tests.

- Have students practice giving, listening to, and following verbal and written directions. The language used in some standardized test directions, for example, may be more formal than what your students are accustomed to.

- Show your students sample copies of standardized tests, if possible, or provide examples of the various formats used on tests. Familiarity with various formats can help students concentrate on the test questions.

- Give students timed and untimed practice tests (or parts of tests) to expose them to the procedures and test conditions they can expect. This will help students get used to working without teacher guidance and within specified time limits, and it will also help reduce their anxiety levels.

For Grades 1.3–6, HOUGHTON MIFFLIN READING provides these additional resources on test-taking:

- The Taking Tests feature at the end of each theme in the Anthology gives students tips and strategies for answering various types of test questions.

- The corresponding pages at the end of each theme in the *Teacher's Edition* include additional test-taking strategies to share with students. (Grades 2–6: See Monitoring Student Progress at the end of each theme in the Teacher's Edition.)

- The *Practice Book* provides test practice pages that correspond to the question format covered in each theme.

The *Integrated Theme Tests*, the *Theme Skills Tests*, and the *Benchmark Progress Tests* available with HOUGHTON MIFFLIN READING give students practice with certain standardized test formats as well as assess students' skills.

- Tell students that they should feel free to mark up their test booklets in any way that is helpful to them—for example,

  - underlining keywords or clues in questions;
  - underlining possible answers in passages;
  - jotting notes or ideas in the booklet margins;
  - check-marking questions they want to return to later;
  - marking their answers in the booklet before marking the answer sheet;
  - crossing out answer choices they know are wrong.

- Have students practice filling in answer sheets, showing them how to

  - complete personal information accurately;
  - match bubble rows to test questions;
  - darken answer bubbles fully and neatly;
  - fill in written responses in the appropriate spaces;
  - keep their place as they record their answers;
  - write complete answers to open-ended questions.

SPECIFIC FORMATS AND QUESTION TYPES

Two common standardized reading test formats consist of a passage followed by a series of (a) multiple-choice questions or (b) open-response questions. Give students the following strategies for tackling test questions of either type.

- Read the questions before reading the passage. Previewing the questions can help you find the answers quickly.

- Always look in the passage to find the answers. Never rely solely on what you already know about a topic.

Multiple-Choice Questions

The following are among the most effective ways to approach multiple-choice questions on standardized tests. Share these strategies with students.

- Answer the easiest questions first. If a question seems difficult, skip it and return to it later.

- Read each question and all its answer choices carefully before choosing the one you think is best. Be sure you understand what the question is really asking.

- Be careful! Wrong answers often contain words or details that match words or details in the passage. Also remember that correct answers may include words that are unfamiliar to you.

- Eliminate answer choices that you know are wrong.

- Mark in your test booklet any answers you're not sure of. Then use any time you have at the end to recheck those answers. Change an answer only if you are sure the first answer is wrong.

- Ask the test monitor whether guessing is penalized. Some tests don't take off points for wrong answers. Others subtract only fractions of points, in which case making an "educated guess" is better than leaving the answer blank.

Open-Response Questions

Open-response questions typically require written answers of varying lengths. Short-response questions might require one to three sentences, and extended-response questions might require a paragraph. Open-response questions often present a special challenge because of their writing and critical thinking aspects. To build students' confidence, give them frequent practice with test items of this type.

Students will also benefit from knowing the kinds of open-response questions they can expect on standardized tests. Explain that open-response questions generally fall into these three categories:

- **Search-and-Find Questions** Answers for these questions are details found right in the passage. Students simply have to find the details and write them down. Here is an example of this type of question: *What happened just after the main character returned home?*

- **Connect-the-Clues Questions** To answer these questions, students must find details in the passage—sometimes in more than one place—and connect them. Here are some sample connect-the-clues questions:

  - *What were two effects of the hurricane?*

  - *How did the survivors feel after the hurricane? Use details from the passage to support your answer.*

- **Stand-Back Questions** In their answers to these questions, students must draw conclusions or express their thoughts about the passage as a whole or about important parts of it. They must also use passage details to support their thoughts. Present these examples of stand-back questions:

  - *What was the author's purpose for writing the passage? Use details from the passage to explain your answer.*

  - *Write a summary of the passage's main points.*

Teacher's Note

- Model test-taking strategies for your students. Try answering the questions yourself to see what strategies you find most valuable, and then have students answer the same questions. Discuss the strategies that you and the students found most and least helpful.

- Have students explain why they answered each question as they did. Explore incorrect answer choices as well, to help students understand distracters.

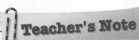

Teacher's Note

Spend some time observing your students as they take standardized tests or practice tests. Take notes on the strategies you see students using and on their behavioral responses to the stresses of test-taking. Use those observations to fine-tune your future instruction on test-taking strategies.

Teacher's Note

Writing Prompts

- Give students practice reading prompts to find the topic and writing type.

- For some prompts have students plan or map out their responses but not actually write them; discuss planned responses as a class.

- For some prompts have students plan a response and write only the introduction or write a complete paper.

Encourage your students to use the following strategies when answering open-response questions.

- Plan the time you'll spend answering each type of question. Spend less time answering short-response questions and more time answering extended-response questions, depending on the total time allowed.

- *Use* your test booklet. Underline keywords and details in the questions; then match them with keywords and details in the passage.

- Make notes in the booklet; use your notes to organize your answers.

- In your answers, include keywords from the questions and details and precise words from the passage.

- Don't write too much! Write only enough to answer the question.

- Don't leave any question unanswered. Answer every one, even the hard ones, as well as you can.

- If a question has more than one part, answer all parts.

- Be sure to show your work (notes and outlines, for example) if the test directions ask you to do so.

- Answer in complete sentences. Pay close attention to spelling, punctuation, and capitalization.

- Use your best handwriting.

Writing Prompts

Many states administer writing tests that require students to write a composition responding to a prompt. The best way to help students prepare for such tests is to give them plenty of experience with the writing process in various modes: expository, narrative, persuasive, and so on. You can also teach them strategies for reading prompts and for planning responses.

These strategies can help students get the information they need from a writing prompt.

- Read the entire prompt carefully.

- Look for words in the prompt that tell the topic of your composition—for example, *school uniforms*, *an unexpected visitor*, or *a talking dog*.

- Look for words in the prompt that help you know which type of writing to use.

  - Sometimes the prompt tells the type of writing—for example, *Write a story about . . . .*

  - Sometimes the prompt simply gives clues. Words like *convince* or *persuade*, for example, suggest that you need to write a persuasive essay.

These strategies can help students plan a response to a writing prompt.

- Think about the key parts of the type of writing you will use. For example, a persuasive essay has a statement of the writer's goal or purpose, reasons that support the goal or purpose statement, and details (facts and examples) that support each reason. A story has at least one character, a setting, and events that are usually told in time order.

- Brainstorm ideas for each key part. Write notes on your test booklet.

- Use the best ideas from your brainstorming to write a rough plan or outline for your composition.

- If the test includes time to revise, look back over your work, keeping the key parts in mind, and make revisions.

- Hand in all your prewriting notes if you are required to do so.

BEATING STRESS AND ANXIETY

It's normal for students to be anxious on the day of a test. They will feel a lot of pressure to perform well. Students who usually work slowly may panic when they must work within a test's time limits. By doing the following, you can help to minimize the stress and anxiety your students experience when they take standardized tests.

- If students are nervous, tell them that nearly everyone is nervous before a test. Point out that this test is only one measure of their achievement. Emphasize the fact that no one is expected to know how to answer every single test question correctly.

- Teach students some simple relaxation techniques, such as closing their eyes and taking a few deep, slow breaths, stretching in their seats, or rolling their heads around to reduce tightness in their necks and shoulders.

Internet

Tech Tip

Benchmark papers, rubrics, and scoring analyses for the major types of writing taught in the Reading-Writing Workshop can be reached through the online teachers' pages for Houghton Mifflin Reading: http://eduplace.com/rdg/hmr. Click on Professional Development.

As testing day nears, enlist the help of the students' parents. Tell them the date of the test. Ask them to see that students get plenty of sleep the night before the test and eat properly on the morning of the test. Also ask them to help students get to the test early and with any materials they will need. Finally, you may want to give the parents pointers about easing their children's nervousness.

- Use practice tests to help students become comfortable with the test procedures and formats. Practice tests will also help students learn to pace themselves while paying attention to time limits.

- Just before the test begins, engage the class in a fun activity to take their minds off the test. You might, for example, list some everyday objects on the board, erase the list, and challenge students to recall and name all of the objects that were listed.

Understanding Standardized Tests

Keep in mind that standardized tests are just one part of a balanced assessment program. In general, they are better used for overall program evaluation than for evaluation of individual students.

FOUR TYPES OF TESTS

A **norm-referenced** test is based on the performance of a national cross-section of students. A student's score reflects his or her performance as compared to this norming, or "standardizing," group—not to the students in your classroom or even in your town. Norm-referenced tests are best used as broad measures of achievement, so they would not necessarily be useful to you for making specific instructional decisions.

A **criterion-referenced** test is designed to measure a student's performance against pre-established standards, not against the performance of a norming group. This definition has been traditionally associated with skills tests, but it can apply to any assessment. On a criterion-referenced test of one hundred items, for example—whether it is testing vocabulary skills or comprehension—mastery might be defined by a score of 80 percent correct.

A related type of test is a **standards-based assessment**. Many states publish content standards, sometimes called *outcomes* or *frameworks*, for what students should know and be able to do at specified grade levels or grade-level bands. The assessments are specifically designed to align with these content standards. Performance standards (criteria) are also set to determine whether or not students have learned the content standards. Many statewide tests are designed to reflect both state content standards and performance standards.

A **diagnostic test** is specifically designed to show areas of strength and weakness in individual children and to help you plan instruction.

NORM-REFERENCED TEST SCORES

The number of test items a student answers correctly becomes his or her raw score, which is then translated into more comparative information.

- A **percentile rank** shows where the student's score falls in relation to a comparable group in the norming population. A percentile rank of 64 on a national reading assessment, for example, means that the student reads as well as or better than 64 percent of the students who made up the population on which the test was standardized. It does *not* mean that the student correctly answered 64 percent of the questions. Similarly, a percentile rank of 50 represents average performance at the tested grade level. It is *not* a failing score.

- A **stanine score** places a student's performance in one of nine bands (*stanine* is short for *standard nine*). Each stanine includes a wide range of raw scores. The most important thing to know is that most students fall within stanines 4–6 and that a score drop or increase of two or more stanines is a clear indication of a change for the worse or the better.

- **Grade-equivalent scores** and **age-equivalent scores** reflect the projected scores of average students at specific points in a school year (say, Grade 4.3—third month of fourth grade) or at specific ages (say, age 9.2— nine years, two months) on a test for a certain grade level (say, Grade 4). If a fourth-grader earns a grade-equivalent score of 7.2 on a national reading assessment, for example, you cannot assume that the student could read seventh-grade books. The 7.2 score represents what an average student two months into the seventh grade might score on the *fourth*-grade test. In other words, the score tells you what you probably already know based on your ongoing informal assessment—that your fourth-grader reads very well.

It is important for teachers to educate students and their parents about what standardized tests measure and how they are weighed along with other assessments teachers use. Both students and parents need to know that these tests are just one part of your assessment program.

Using Assessment to Reach All Learners

Introduction

Meeting individual needs in today's diverse classrooms is one of the most challenging aspects of a teacher's job. HOUGHTON MIFFLIN READING includes many supports—detailed in Program Resources boxes throughout this handbook and in the charts completing Parts 4, 5, and 7—that help you customize instruction for all your students. Extra Support and Challenge modifications and activities can at different times be used for various populations in your class—including the two special populations discussed here: English language learners and students with special needs. The goal of Part 9 is to alert you to program resources that will help you not only assess these students but also tailor instruction so that they can progress along with the rest of your class.

English Language Learners

If you have English language learners (ELL) in your classroom (and whether or not they receive special instruction outside of your classroom), your teaching and assessment jobs have an added dimension: those students' level of English acquisition. The task of assessment becomes threefold: to measure a student's language acquisition; to measure his or her grasp of concepts, strategies, and skills; and to gauge the effectiveness of your instruction.

It is likely that the students acquiring English in your classroom will be at varying levels of language acquisition: beginning/ preproduction, early production, speech-emergent, and intermediate/advanced or fluent.

You will need to tailor both instruction and assessment for students at each level. The Student Profiles on pages 80–81 provide a glimpse of demonstrable student behaviors at each language-proficiency level for four areas: listening, speaking, reading, and writing.

TEACHING AND ASSESSMENT TECHNIQUES

HOUGHTON MIFFLIN READING includes built-in supports before, during, and after each reading selection so that all learners, including your English language learners, can be successful with the program (see Modifying

Instruction, on page 83). In both instructional and assessment activities, you—and your students, depending on their proficiency level—can use these additional techniques to overcome immediate communication barriers as you work together.

- Use pictures and props or point to objects.

- Use pantomime, role-playing, or posing.

- Use picture/word cards for different concepts (cause and effect, for example).

- Use "quick draw" for different concepts or to show story sequence.

- Use chants, songs, and games.

- Use graphic organizers.

- Use sentence strips.

- Let students dictate stories and test answers.

- Use dialogue tapes or journals. If you can manage it, carrying on these running spoken or written "conversations" with your students acquiring English will not only help students to expand their speaking and writing skills but will provide records of their progress over time.

ONGOING INFORMAL ASSESSMENT

You can informally assess your students acquiring English in much the same way as you assess your English-proficient students, but keep these special considerations in mind.

- If a student's response is insufficient or inappropriate, try rephrasing your question or request.

- Watch for nonverbal clues, such as body language and facial expressions, to assess comprehension in students at the preproduction level.

- Observe students in classroom situations they find most comfortable. For example, a student may feel more relaxed in a small group than in a large group.

The English Language Learners Checklists on pages 118–123 of this handbook are blackline masters that you can use to measure a student's progress toward a higher language-proficiency level. Use the checklists at regular intervals, but don't feel that you must check all categories during each observation.

STUDENT PROFILE: KINDERGARTEN

Criterion	Beginning/ Preproduction	Early Production	Speech Emergent	Intermediate/ Advanced Fluency	Fluent
Listening	Student comprehends simple repeated sentences; follows simple directions; shows comprehension through facial expressions, body language, and gestures.	Student comprehends simple text; begins to follow group discussions; shows comprehension by using one or two words or short phrases.	Student understands most of what is said; follows stories; follows a series of directions; takes part in discussions; writes from dictation.	Student understands what is said at normal speed, with occasional repetition; follows less predictable stories and nonfiction selections; actively takes part in discussions.	Student understands what is said without any difficulty.
Speaking	Student responds nonverbally, by gesturing (pointing, nodding, choosing), and by imitating sounds and actions.	Student makes short, appropriate oral responses to questions; dictates simple sentences; chimes in with classmates on poems, songs, and chants.	Student speaks in phrases or simple sentences; uses more complex sentence patterns; engages in dialogues and role-plays.	Student engages in conversation approaching fluency; expresses feelings and experiences; presents oral reports; formulates and asks questions.	Student speaks fluently in conversations and group discussions.
Reading	Student follows along in picture walks; uses illustrations and other graphic clues to attach meaning to printed material.	Student begins to chime in during shared readings of predictable texts; supplies next word as teacher pauses while reading familiar text.	Student begins to follow text during group reading; matches words to some objects, people, and actions; retells stories using words, pictures, and objects.	Student reads or recites familiar text; identifies characters; answers questions about main ideas; sequences events; compares/contrasts; shows cause/effect; begins using context and decoding skills to read words.	Student reads aloud familiar texts; answers questions about story elements; makes inferences; predicts outcomes; begins to understand idiomatic expressions.
Writing	Student illustrates objects and events to convey meaning.	Student conveys stories or simple ideas in drawings; may use pictures plus simple symbols to write messages.	Student dictates simple labels for illustrations of objects, characters, and actions; writes own name; uses pictures to complete sentence frames.	Student dictates simple sentences to go with drawings; attempts to write one- or two-word captions; begins writing names of classmates and family members.	Student begins using temporary spelling; attempts writing phrases and sentences; writes for a variety of purposes.

Criterion	Beginning/ Preproduction	Early Production	Speech Emergent	Intermediate/ Advanced Fluency	Fluent
Listening	Student comprehends simple repeated sentences; follows simple directions; shows comprehension through facial expressions, body language, and gestures.	Student comprehends simple text; begins to follow group discussions; shows comprehension by using one or two words or short phrases.	Student understands most of what is said; follows stories; follows a series of directions; takes part in discussions; writes from dictation.	Student understands what is said at normal speed, with occasional repetition; follows complex stories and nonfiction selections; actively takes part in discussions.	Student understands what is said without any difficulty.
Speaking	Student responds nonverbally, by gesturing (pointing, nodding, choosing), and by imitating sounds and actions.	Student makes short, appropriate oral responses to questions; dictates simple sentences; recites poems, songs, and chants.	Student speaks in phrases or simple sentences; uses more complex sentence patterns; engages in dialogues, interviews, and role-plays.	Student engages in conversation approaching fluency; expresses feelings and experiences; presents oral reports; formulates and asks questions.	Student speaks fluently in conversations and group discussions; has no trouble expressing opinions; shows appropriate use of English idioms.
Reading	Student follows along in picture walks; uses illustrations and other graphic clues to attach meaning to printed material.	Student follows text during group reading; matches words to some objects, people, and actions; retells stories using pictures and objects.	Student reads aloud; identifies characters; identifies main ideas; sequences events; compares/contrasts; shows cause/effect; uses context and decoding skills to find word meanings.	Student reads aloud and silently; identifies story elements; makes inferences; predicts outcomes; summarizes selections; begins to recognize idiomatic expressions.	Student has full command of reading strategies; acquires and applies information from various genres; selects and reads materials of personal interest.
Writing	Student illustrates objects and events to convey meaning.	Student labels illustrations of objects, people, and actions; writes familiar names and simple words; uses temporary spelling, rebuses, and illustrations to convey ideas.	Student writes from dictation; writes simple sentences; uses details; completes cloze and story frames; demonstrates writing as a process; uses a variety of genres	Student paraphrases; writes to persuade, inform, and describe; relates reading and personal experiences; uses conventions of grammar and mechanics.	Student writes in greater detail in a wider variety of genres for a wider variety of purposes.

Program Resources

The *Handbook for English Language Learners* contains lessons for every selection in each theme of HOUGHTON MIFFLIN READING. In addition, the *Teacher's Edition* contains numerous suggestions for adapting various activities. See Modifying Instruction on page 83 of this handbook.

Using the Leveled Reading Passages

Because it contains reading passages at many different levels, you will be able to use the *Leveled Reading Passages Assessment Kit* with students at the speech-emergent stage and above. The kit helps you evaluate students' phonics and decoding skills; reading rate, accuracy, and fluency; reading comprehension; and use of reading strategies.

Using Portfolios

If you use portfolios in your classroom, your English language learners can keep them in the same way that your English-proficient students do. If you don't, be sure to maintain a collection of artifacts from your English language learners. The contents will reflect the instructional methods and materials you use with these students. For example, if you use the specialized lessons in the *Handbook for English Language Learners,* you may want to include one dated sample of a student's writing or drawing for each selection's lessons. Samples may consist of sentence strips, story frames, word webs, dictated stories, and picture-word cards. You may also wish to include one English Language Learners Checklist (pages 118–123) per theme and cassettes with samples of a student's oral reading, retelling, or speaking at different times during the year. Assembled in a portfolio, these materials create an authentic picture of each student's readiness to move to the next language-proficiency level and level of mastery of the concepts, skills, and strategies you have been working on.

Student Self-Assessment

Although they may not realize it as such, English language learners engage in self-assessment regularly. Language acquisition provides all sorts of external indicators of progress: when students can go into a store and purchase something by name, they know they have made progress. In the classroom you can reinforce their awareness—in teacher-student conferences, for example.

Another way you can help students monitor their own progress over time is by having them compare early and recent tapes and other work samples from their portfolios. The benefit of portfolios for these students is that they can chart their own development rather than comparing themselves to English-proficient classmates. With modeling from you and practice, they can begin to set, say, weekly goals based on a review of their portfolios. The goals can be few and basic—completing a piece of writing or using a particular reading strategy—but they allow students to take charge of an aspect of their learning and provide them with milestones for self-assessment.

FORMAL ASSESSMENT

The formal assessment measures in HOUGHTON MIFFLIN READING may be appropriate for your English language learners, depending on the students' level of language acquisition.

- As a general rule, you might want to delay any formal assessment of students until they have reached at least the early production level.

- The *Baseline Test* may be used with speech-emergent, intermediate/advanced, or completely fluent students.

- You may want to administer the *Benchmark Test*, the *Integrated Theme Tests*, and the *Theme Skills Tests* orally for students at the early production and speech-emergent levels. Some students with intermediate/advanced fluency may also need to be tested orally.

- The Teacher's Annotated Edition of the *Integrated Theme Tests* includes for each test a feature called Reaching All Learners. It suggests ways to meet individual needs by giving partial support or full support to students taking the tests. In addition, each test comes in an alternative format: a summary of the reading selection from the full test, plus three multiple-choice questions about the summary.

Please remember that these formal assessment measures should not be your sole means of assessing English language learners. Further, if the tests are not appropriate for your students or helpful to you, you might want to concentrate on informal assessment methods.

MODIFYING INSTRUCTION

The modifications you might make for your English language learners based on assessment will involve providing extra support or challenge as described throughout this handbook—with the added requirement of taking into account students' levels of language acquisition. HOUGHTON MIFFLIN READING also includes resources that will help you meet this additional need.

- The *Get Set for Reading* CD-ROM contains interactive background-building and vocabulary activities for each selection in the Anthology. The activities are also available in Spanish—at the click of a button. *Get Set for Reading* can be used with an adaptive keyboard that enables students with motor or visual impairments to access these activities.

- Reaching All Learners support boxes for English Language Learners throughout the *Teacher's Edition* help you provide specialized support.

Program Resources

- A Managing Flexible Groups chart in the Teacher's Edition helps you plan support each week.

- The *Classroom Management Handbook*, which includes selection-related independent activities, helps you organize time and materials to facilitate work with groups.

- The *Challenge Handbook*, which contains activities and projects for your most advanced students, can be used in connection with the *Classroom Management Handbook*.

- Audios of all reading selections in the Anthology support students as they read.

- The *Handbook for English Language Learners* contains summaries of every selection in HOUGHTON MIFFLIN READING. The summaries are written in simpler language and in a simpler narrative style than the selections. The handbook also contains lessons for every selection that include multi-level response questions and multi-level skill practice. The *Classroom Intervention Kit*, available with the program, contains the handbook and also picture word cards, blackline masters for each week's lessons, and transparencies of the teacher Read Alouds (the extra pieces are blackline masters in the handbook).

- An annotated Leveled Bibliography of Leveled Books for Independent Reading begins each theme in the *Teacher's Edition*.

- The Phonics Library, for Grades 1–2, is a collection of easy vocabulary-controlled reading selections; the Language Support Leveled Readers (Grades 1–6) and the easy Theme Paperbacks at each grade are easy-to-read books on the selection or theme topic.

Students with Special Needs

Your classroom may include a number of students with special needs because of learning, physical, or other disabilities. Some of these students may have individual education programs (IEPs) and may also have special classroom aides who help them with some or all of their subjects. These students may also spend part of the day with a special education teacher outside of the classroom. Whether or not your students with special needs have extra resources, you will need to tailor instruction and assessment for them. Always keep in mind that you must bring these students back to and involve them in the general curriculum as much as possible and whenever they need to move away from it for extra support.

INSTRUCTIONAL TECHNIQUES

There are several methods you can use to help your students with special needs access and make progress in the general education curriculum.

- Give them additional instruction. Put students in small groups for extra work with you on areas that are especially difficult. (Students who do not have documented special needs may also benefit from this type of group work.)

- Build background for reading experiences by preteaching concepts, vocabulary, reading strategies, and so on; provide selection summaries to help students before and as they read.

- Provide opportunities for repeated reading of familiar texts. (This is especially important for students who decode successfully but do not read fluently.)

- Have students read with partners.

- Present material in smaller chunks.

- Have students work with peer tutors on the application of skills. Working on assignments with partners can benefit both the "teaching" student, who must conceptualize and impart the information, and the "learning" student, who is given one-on-one help with approaches and strategies he or she might not have been able to apply alone.

- Use scaffolding resources or alternative paths through material that the whole class is learning. For example, audios help students as they read, and easier reading selections allow students to read successfully while learning the same strategies and skills as the rest of the class.

- Give students printed copies of instructions and assignments you give orally so that they can refer to them later.

- Use multisensory approaches: oral explanations and read-alouds, visuals, graphic organizers, manipulatives, and so on.

- If you use a reading intervention program with your students with special needs, use it in addition to your regular language-arts instruction with these students.

- Co-plan instruction with the special education teacher or specialist in your school or district. He or she may be able to suggest approaches to use with your particular students.

Home/Community Connection

Involving Parents

- If you give assignments that students must finish or work on at home, you might want to mail a list of those assignments to parents.

- If possible, schedule regular parent-teacher conferences.

ONGOING INFORMAL ASSESSMENT

You can informally assess your students with special needs in much the same way you do the rest of your class. As with all your students, the goal of ongoing informal assessment is twofold: to monitor student progress and to gauge instructional effectiveness.

- Observe these students often so that you can fine-tune your instruction. For example, as you map out the observations that you'll do using checklists, rotate your students with special needs through the list more frequently than other students.

- Have conferences with these students more often. Work with students to set short-term goals, and follow up on those goals during your next conference.

Program Resources

Several assessments available with HOUGHTON MIFFLIN READING are suitable for students with special needs, both for initial planning and placement and for ongoing informal assessment:

- The *Phonics/Decoding Screening Test* and the *Lexia Quick Phonics Assessment CD-ROM*, for assessing phonemic awareness and phonics/decoding skills

- The *Leveled Reading Passages Assessment Kit*, for assessing oral reading fluency

- Attend your students' IEP meetings, both for assistance in meeting students' IEP goals and objectives and for insight and interchange about the needs of each student.

- Modify other informal assessments as necessary. At Grade 1, for example, you might administer the weekly Alternative Assessment found in the *Teacher's Resource Blackline Masters* instead of taking an Oral Reading Record; at other grade levels, you might administer the Selection Tests individually and orally to some students.

Using Portfolios

If you use portfolios in your classroom, your students with special needs can keep them too. Additionally, your own portfolios for these students can help you chart their progress and note instructional methods and modifications that worked. If you use the specialized lessons in the *Extra Support Handbook* (see page 87), you may want to include dated Practice pages from the comprehension and other Skill Focus lessons.

Student Self-Assessment

In your teacher-student conferences, you can guide your students to concentrate on only one or two things at a time in their self-assessment. You can help them self-assess their strengths as well by drawing attention to what they're good at. Finally, you can help students— and they can help you—learn about how they learn best.

FORMAL ASSESSMENT

Some general modifications to your testing procedures may help your students with special needs. You might allow students to use their books when taking tests; give practice questions; give multiple-choice instead of open-response questions; give the test individually and orally; or give the test in smaller chunks over a couple of days.

With certain modifications the formal assessments in HOUGHTON MIFFLIN READING may be appropriate for your students with special needs. Here are two examples.

- You might give only certain subtests of the *Theme Skills Tests*, depending on how you have tailored instruction. You might also give the test or subtests orally or over more than one day.

- The Teacher's Annotated Edition of the *Integrated Theme Tests* includes for each test a feature called Reaching All Learners. It suggests ways to give partial or full support to students taking the tests. In addition, each test comes in an alternative format: a summary of the reading selection from the full test, plus simplified questions about the summary.

One of the principles of fair testing practices for students with special needs—and indeed for all students—is that assessments reflect instruction. That is, students should not be tested on material that is not part of their school's and their class's curriculum. To that end, you need to work with the special-education teachers who develop the IEP objectives for your students with special needs. If you plan to use the *Integrated Theme Tests* or the *Theme Skills Tests*, for example, make sure that the special-education teachers know what those tests entail. Conversely, learning about accommodations for testing that have been established by each student's IEP team will help you decide how further to modify the tests you give in your class.

MODIFYING INSTRUCTION

HOUGHTON MIFFLIN READING contains numerous resources to help you teach your students with special needs.

- The *Get Set for Reading* CD-ROM contains interactive background-building and vocabulary activities for each selection in the Anthology. The CD-ROM can be used with an adaptive keyboard that enables students with motor or visual impairments to access these activities.

- Selection summaries in the *Teacher's Resource Blackline Masters* and audios of all reading selections in the Anthology support students before and as they read.

- The *Extra Support Handbook* contains preteaching and reteaching lessons, as well as literature previews, for every Anthology selection. Teaching and student Practice blackline masters are also included.

- For students who are able to read the Anthology selections, Extra Support/Intervention boxes throughout each selection provide useful approaches.

- Monitoring Student Progress in the Reteaching lessons give you additional approaches to try with students who are struggling with skills.

- The Phonics Library, for Grades 1–2, is a collection of easy vocabulary-controlled reading selections; the Language Support Leveled Readers (Grades 1–6) and the below level Theme Paperbacks at each grade are easy-to-read books on the selection or theme topic.

- An annotated Leveled Bibliography of Leveled Books for Independent Reading (Books for Small-Group Reading at Grade 1.1–1.2) begins of each theme in the *Teacher's Edition*.

Part 10

Blackline Masters

How to Use the Blackline Masters

On the following pages you will find reproducible checklists, forms, inventories, and guides to use as you plan instruction, prepare for student and parent conferences, observe students, and help students with the assessment process. You will complete some of the forms, while students will complete or refer to others. You may want to keep some checklists and forms in your evaluation notebook and store others in student portfolios.

As you will see, several of the checklists can be used on an individual or a group basis. If you want to use a checklist for an individual student, write the student's name at the top of the page and fill in the observation date above each column. To use the checklist with a group, simply fill in the observation date at the top of the page and write student names above the columns. Samples of completed individual and group checklists appear to the left.

If you are using a group checklist, make as many copies as you will need to record observations for each student. For example, for the Listening, Speaking, and Viewing Checklist shown to the left and located on page 108 of this handbook, six columns appear. If you have eighteen students in your class, then you will need three copies of the checklist.

Listening/Speaking/Viewing Checklist
(Individual)

Listening/Speaking/Viewing Checklist
(Group)

Contents

Assessment Planning Guide

This guide is designed to help you select assessment activities that fit with your instructional goals.

Beginning of the Year

- Student interviews
- *Baseline Group Test*
- *Emerging Literacy Survey* (K–2)
- *Phonics/Decoding Screening Test* (1–6)
- *Lexia Quick Phonics Assessment CD-ROM*

- *Leveled Reading Passages Assessment Kit*
- Student Interest Inventory
- Reading Attitudes and Habits Inventory
  (Try to use at least once more during the term.)
- Attitudes and Habits Inventory (Early/Fluent Writer)
  (Try to use at least once more during the term.)

Per Week

- Teacher-student conferences
  (five or six students a week)
- Informal Assessment Checklist
  (five or six students a week)

- Anecdotal notes
  (all students at least once a week)
- Student self-assessment time
  (every one or two weeks)

Per Term

- Teacher-parent conference
  (one or two times a year)
- *Benchmark Progress Test*
  (two or three times a year)
- *Integrated Theme Test* (one per theme)
- *Theme Skills Test* (one per theme)
- Fluent Reader Checklist
  (one or two times per term)
- Kindergarten Observation Checklists
  (three times per term, observing five or six
  students at a time)
- Listening, Speaking, and Viewing Checklist
  (three times per term, observing five or six
  students at a time)

- Oral Reading Checklist (three times
  per term, observing five or six students at a time)
- Reading Attitudes and Habits Inventory
  (at least once after initial use, to show progress
  during term)
- Writing Attitudes and Habits Inventory
  (at least once after initial use, to show progress
  during term)
- Portfolios (Review and have students review
  one or two times per term. Use for evaluation
  once per term.)
- Oral Reading Record/Leveled Reading Passages
  (one or two times per term, as necessary)
- English Language Learners Checklist
  (one or two times per term)

End of the Year

- Teacher-parent conference
- Portfolio review

- *Benchmark Progress Test*
- Final evaluation for report cards

Student Interest Inventory

Write your answers, or draw them on another piece of paper.

Name_____

1. In school my favorite things to do are _____

_____

_____

_____

_____

2. Outside of school, I like to _____

_____

_____

_____

3. At home I like to read _____

_____

_____

_____

_____

4. I like to write _____

_____

_____

_____

5. My two favorite books are _____

_____

_____

_____

6. My favorite author is _____

_____

7. When I am an adult, I want to _____

_____

_____

_____

Self Reflection/Self-Assessment

Name _____

At different times during the year,
rate yourself on these items.

– = No/Never			
√ = Maybe/Sometimes			
√+ = Yes/Always			

Thinking About My Reading					
I like stories.					
I like nonfiction.					
I read a variety of materials (books, newspapers, magazines).					
I talk with others about what I am reading.					
I choose my reading topics.					
I think my reading is improving.					
Thinking About My Writing					
I write in class and at home.					
I write in different forms (story, letter, personal narrative).					
I pick my own writing topics.					
I revise my writing carefully.					
I listen to other people's suggestions for my writing.					
I share my writing with the class.					
I share my writing at home.					
I think my writing is improving.					

Evaluating and Setting Goals for Myself

On the back of this sheet, write today's date and your answers to these questions: How have you changed as a reader? as a writer? What are three things that you need to work on as a reader? as a writer?

Concepts of Print and Book Handling

Kindergarten Observation Checklist

For individual use, write the name on the line above and dates of observations between the slanted lines. For group use, write students' names between the slanted lines.

– = Beginning	√ = Developing
√+ = Proficient	

Concepts of Print						
Is aware of print in the environment						
Understands that spoken language can be written down						
Knows that print is read top to bottom, left to right, with return sweep						
Understands the concept of "letter"						
Understands the concepts of "word" and "spaces"						
Understands the concept of "sentence"						
Matches spoken words to print						
Is aware of different purposes of print (e.g., information, enjoyment)						
Book Handling						
Holds the book right-side up						
Understands, can find title						
Understands, can find author						
Turns pages in sequence						
Moves from the front to the back of the book						

Comments: _____

_____

_____

Phonemic Awareness and Phonics

Kindergarten Observation Checklist

For individual use, write the name on the line above and dates of observations between the slanted lines. For group use, write students' names between the slanted lines.

– = Beginning	√ = Developing
√+ = Proficient	

Phonemic Awareness						
Recognizes rhyming words						
Identifies beginning sounds						
Identifies syllables in spoken words						
Blends onsets and rimes						
Identifies words in oral sentences						
Segments onsets and rimes						
Blends phonemes						
Blends and segments phonemes						
Substitutes phonemes						
Phonics						
Recognizes sound(s) for consonant(s) _____						
Recognizes same consonant sound(s) in final position						
Recognizes sound(s) for consonant(s) _____						
Recognizes same consonant sound(s) in final position						
Builds words with the short vowel family(ies) _____						
Builds words with the short vowel family(ies) _____						
Recognizes final *x*						

Comments: _____

_____

Emerging Reading

Kindergarten Observation Checklist

For individual use, write the name on the line above and dates of observations between the slanted lines. For group use, write students' names between the slanted lines.

– = Beginning √ = Developing √+ = Proficient

Decoding Behaviors and Strategies						
Names letters						
Associates sounds with letters						
Uses phonics skills to decode new words						
Recognizes high-frequency words that have been taught						
Uses context/meaning cues to confirm the identification of unfamiliar words						
Responding to Literature						
Shows enjoyment of literature						
Predicts what will happen next in a story						
Responds to literature with questions and/or comments						
Relates literature to personal knowledge/experience						
Becomes familiar with story elements (characters, events)						
Becomes familiar with text that conveys facts						
Uses theme's comprehension skill						
Rereading of Familiar Storybook						
Makes comments but does not retell story						
Retells the story using pictures						
Uses oral language or appropriate vocabulary						
Uses a mix of oral and story language						
Uses story language						
Tracks print and attempts to read the words						

Emerging Writing

Kindergarten Observation Checklist

For individual use, write the name on the line above
and dates of observations between the slanted lines.
For group use, write students' names between the
slanted lines.

– = Beginning	√ = Developing
	√+ = Proficient

Writing Behaviors						
Contributes to group stories						
Draws to convey meaning						
Prints letters						
Writes own name						
Writes own messages						
Uses correct directional patterns						
Uses spaces between words						
Stages of Spelling Development						
Scribbles or play-writes						
Prints letterlike shapes or random letters						
Writes using beginning consonant sounds						
Represents sounds in middle or end of word						
Uses conventional spelling for some words						

Comments: _____

_____

_____

_____

_____

Oral Language

Kindergarten Observation Checklist

For individual use, write the name on the line above and dates of observations between the slanted lines. For group use, write students' names between the slanted lines.

– = Beginning	√ = Developing
√+ = Proficient	

Listening Attentively						
In individual conferences						
In small groups						
In large groups						
Listening for Information						
Identifies topic						
Recalls specific details						
Recalls events in sequence						
Listening to Directions						
Follows one-step oral directions						
Follows two-step oral directions						
Follows three-step oral directions						
Listening to Books						
Recalls title and author						
Distinguishes between real and make-believe						
Recalls characters						
Recalls events in sequence						
Recalls facts						
Recognizes cause-and-effect relationships						
Recognizes main idea						
Makes judgments						
Predicts outcomes						
Speaking/Language Development						
Seeks to communicate with others						
Expresses ideas clearly						
Exhibits a good vocabulary						
During Conversations and Discussions						
Speaks confidently						
Relates comments to topics						
Shares new ideas						
Thinks before speaking						
Considers other people's feelings and ideas						

Retelling

Kindergarten Observation Checklist

For individual use, write the name on the line above
and dates of observations between the slanted lines.
For group use, write students' names between the
slanted lines.

– = Beginning	√ = Developing
√+ =	Proficient

Retelling						
Shows independence						
Shows accuracy						
Retelling a Story						
Identifies main characters						
Identifies the setting						
Recalls sequence						
Identifies story problem						
Identifies story solution						
Retelling Informational Text						
Identifies overall topic						
Recalls main idea with teacher's help						
Recalls supporting details with teacher's help						
Makes inferences with teacher's help						

Comments: _____

_____

_____

_____

_____

_____

_____

Informal Assessment Checklist (1–2)

Student _____ **Theme** _____

– = Beginning	√ = Developing	√+ = Proficient

	Understanding	Comments
Selection/Week:		
Phonemic Awareness		
Phonics/Decoding		
High-Frequency Words		
Comprehension Skill		
Comprehension Strategy		
Spelling		
Vocabulary Skill		
Writing Skill		
Grammar, Usage, and Mechanics		
Listening, Speaking, and Viewing		
Information and Study Skill		
Selection/Week:		
Phonemic Awareness		
Phonics/Decoding		
High-Frequency Words		
Comprehension Skill		
Comprehension Strategy		
Spelling		
Vocabulary Skill		
Writing Skill		
Grammar, Usage, and Mechanics		
Listening, Speaking, and Viewing		
Information and Study Skill		
General Observation		
Independent Reading		
Independent Writing		
Work Habits		
Self-Assessment		

Comments: _____

_____

Informal Assessment Checklist (3–6)

Student _____   **Theme** _____

– = Beginning	√ = Developing	√+ = Proficient

	Understanding	Comments
Selection:		
Comprehension Strategy		
Comprehension Skill		
Information and Study Skill		
Structural Analysis		
Phonics		
Spelling		
Vocabulary Skill		
Grammar		
Writing Skill		
Listening, Speaking, and Viewing		
Selection:		
Comprehension Strategy		
Comprehension Skill		
Information and Study Skill		
Structural Analysis		
Phonics		
Spelling		
Vocabulary Skill		
Grammar		
Writing Skill		
Listening, Speaking, and Viewing		
General Observation		
Independent Reading		
Independent Writing		
Work Habits		
Self-Assessment		

Comments: _____

_____

_____

Oral Reading Checklist

For individual use, write the name on the line above and dates of observations between the slanted lines. For group use, write students' names between the slanted lines.

– = Beginning √ = Developing √+ = Proficient						
Speaks clearly						
Uses phonics skills to figure out difficult words						
Reads through to the end of sentences						
Pauses at the end of sentences						
Pauses at commas						
Is able to read both narrative and expository texts						
Reads narrative with feeling						
Uses appropriate inflection when reading dialogue						
Reads confidently						

Comments: _____

_____

_____

_____

_____

_____

_____

_____

_____

_____

_____

_____

Oral Reading Record

Student _____

Book _____ Date _____

L.1 _____

L.2 _____

L.3 _____

L.4 _____

L.5 _____

L.6 _____

L.7 _____

L.8 _____

L.9 _____

L.10 _____

L.11 _____

L.12 _____

L.13 _____

L.14 _____

L.15 _____

Reading rate (WCPM) : _____ **Progress:** ☐ Expected ☐ Below expected ☐ Seriously below expected

Decoding accuracy: $\dfrac{\text{Number of words read correctly}}{\text{Number of words in passage}}$ = ____/____ = ____ %

Phrasing and expression score: _____ (See Teacher's Assessment Handbook, page 26.)

Comments: _____

_____

Word-Reading Fluency

mat	dot	quit	flip	this
huge	slow	asked	wisely	chore
can	kit	will	black	when
hunts	boat	brown	berries	thirsty
big	yet	let's	plans	shame
left	took	cloud	painful	lightest
ran	zig	grabs	knock	think
silk	chew	squealed	rusty	moister
hit	rug	naps	scrub	bike
creek	glue	notes	lawn	larger
pig	van	Jill's	wrist	sand
cried	frowned	sauce	morning	playing
sit	patch	picking	yelled	trail
food	sighed	string	boxes	purred

Letter-Naming Fluency

S	m	R	t	s	B
r	n	H	v	C	a
M	T	N	h	b	V
A	c	S	R	m	t
P	g	f	L	K	q
G	F	l	p	Q	i
K	D	Z	x	d	O
I	X	w	Z	o	y
W	e	j	u	Y	t
J	U	d	E	b	A

Fluent Reader Checklist

For individual use, write the name on the line above and dates of observations between the slanted lines. For group use, write students' names between the slanted lines.

– = Beginning √ = Developing
√+ = Proficient

Integrates reading strategies effectively						
Has a large sight-word vocabulary						
Uses phonics/decoding strategies to decode new words						
Understands text when reading silently						
Reads and comprehends short chapter books						
Uses pictures to confirm and enhance understanding of text						
Reads and comprehends longer chapter books						
Recognizes different characters' points of view in a story						
Reads and comprehends informational selections						
Uses different reading strategies for different text types						
Can read different types of text across the curriculum						
Chooses appropriate books for various purposes						
Reads a variety of sources to research a topic, as appropriate						

Comments: _____

_____

_____

_____

Reading Strategies Checklist

For individual use, write the name on the line above and dates of observations between the slanted lines. For group use, write students' names between the slanted lines.

| – = Beginning | √ = Developing |
| √+ = Proficient | |

Predict/Infer						
Looks for main ideas						
Looks at pictures						
Thinks about prior knowledge						
Thinks about what will happen						
Self-Question						
Asks self questions and tries to find the answers as he/she reads						
Think About Words						
Figures out new words by using ■ sounds ■ word parts ■ context (what makes sense) ■ picture clues						
Monitor						
Asks self if what he/she is reading makes sense						
If not, he/she . . . ■ rereads, aloud or silently ■ looks at the pictures, then ■ asks for help						
Summarize						
Summarizes during reading						
Summarizes after reading						
■ for fiction, thinks about story parts or makes a story map						
■ for nonfiction, thinks about main ideas and details						
Evaluate						
Asks self whether he/she likes the selection						
Asks self whether he/she agrees with ideas or characters						
Compares and contrasts selection with others he/she has read						

Response to Literature Checklist

For individual use, write the name on the line above and dates of observations between the slanted lines. For group use, write students' names between the slanted lines.

– = Beginning	√ = Developing
√+ = Proficient	

Written or Oral Response						
Identifies the selection's elements and structure (beginning, middle, end; introduction, problem/conflict, development, solution)						
Interprets author's intent						
Identifies selection's major themes and issues						
Identifies a selection's or a character's point of view						
Uses evidence from a story to identify a character's traits, feelings, and personality						
Relates characters, places, events, and/or information in a selection to prior knowledge or personal experiences						
Identifies elements of writer's craft in selection (e.g., similes, metaphors, vivid language, humorous elements, symbolism, flashbacks, personification, sarcasm, elements of mood, suspense, and pacing)						
Compares selections to other genres or other pieces of literature						
Expresses personal feelings inspired by the selection						
Supports own interpretations and opinions with references to text and/or own experience						
Uses selection to gain insight into own life and the lives of others						
Discussion Behaviors						
Participates in discussions about the selection						
Listens to others' ideas, adds to their comments						
Suggests relevant new ideas						
Supports ideas with references to text						
Revises or expands on interpretation as discussion progresses						

Listening, Speaking, and Viewing Checklist

For individual use, write the name on the line above and dates of observations between the slanted lines. For group use, write students' names between the slanted lines.

| – = Beginning | √ = Developing |
| √+ = Proficient | |

Speaking						
Volunteers for speaking activities						
Participates in discussions						
Speaks clearly and at an appropriate rate						
Expresses ideas clearly and logically						
Uses prior knowledge appropriately						
Shows vocabulary development in everyday speech						
Speaks in turn during discussions						
Listening						
Pays attention when others speak						
Listens without interrupting						
Shows understanding of what others say						
Follows directions						
Ignores distractions						
Viewing						
Keeps purpose in mind while viewing						
Interprets information from images or visuals						
Evaluates information from images or visuals						
Scans images or visuals in a systematic way						
Reads captions to understand illustrations and other visuals						

Comments: _____

_____

_____

Reading Attitudes and Habits Inventory

For individual use, write the name on the line above and dates of observations between the slanted lines. For group use, write students' names between the slanted lines.

– = Beginning √ = Developing
√+ = Proficient

Enjoys reading					
Reads both fiction and nonfiction					
Reads about a variety of subjects					
Chooses a variety of different reading materials					
Takes out books to read at home					
Likes to find new things to read					
Gets help from the teacher when necessary					
Is able to read with a minimum of help					
Shows confidence in reading					
Discusses reading with friends					
Is willing to read things that others suggest					
Likes being read to					
Has a favorite author or subject					
Has a favorite time and/or place to read					

Comments: _____

_____

_____

_____

_____

Attitudes and Habits Inventory (Early Writer)

For individual use, write the name on the line above and dates of observations between the slanted lines. For group use, write students' names between the slanted lines.

– = Beginning	√ = Developing
√+ = Proficient	

The Writing Process						
Can write in different modes						
Chooses topic independently						
Follows a logical pattern (e.g., beginning, middle, end)						
Elaborates with relevant details						
Matches illustrations to text						
Revises effectively						
Uses beginning proofreading skills						
Shares writing with others						
Thinks of self as an author						
Concepts of Print; Grammar, Usage, and Mechanics						
Writes left to right, top to bottom consistently						
Spaces words correctly						
Uses complete sentences						
Uses correct end punctuation						
Varies sentence structure						
Uses capitals at the beginning of sentences						
Makes subjects and verbs agree						
Uses consistent verb tense						
Spelling						
Uses conventional spelling for most words						
Attempts to spell difficult words						
Uses resources to check spelling						

Attitudes and Habits Inventory (Fluent Writer)

For individual use, write the name on the line above and dates of observations between the slanted lines. For group use, write students' names between the slanted lines.

– = Beginning   √ = Developing
√+ = Proficient

The Writing Process						
Writes well in various modes						
Chooses own topic						
Uses research resources when necessary						
Summarizes information in own words						
Uses vivid language						
Elaborates with relevant details						
Uses a logical organization						
Creates a complete first draft						
Initiates revision						
Willingly shares writing in peer conferences						
Willingly gives and receives advice						
Uses proofreading marks						
Shares finished work						
Grammar, Usage, and Mechanics						
Writes in complete sentences						
Uses correct end punctuation						
Uses commas properly						
Uses quotation marks correctly						
Uses appropriate capitalization						
Uses appropriate pronouns						
Uses correct verb tense						
Makes subjects and verbs agree						
Varies sentence structure						
Uses paragraphs correctly						
Spelling						
Spells most words correctly						
Attempts to spell difficult words						
Uses resources to check spelling						

General Analytic Writing Traits Scoring Sheet

Student's Name _____

Directions: Circle the score for each category. Use suggested weights if desired. Add the scores or total scores to determine the overall score.

Trait	Score	Total	Teacher Comments
Ideas and Content • The ideas are clear, fresh, and/or original. • The writing is focused. • The writing holds the reader's attention. • The main ideas support the topic. • The details support the main ideas.	1 2 3 4 5 x 4		
Organization • The beginning is engaging. • The writing shows clear organization. • Details are logically organized. • Transitional words are used. • The conclusion or ending is strong.	1 2 3 4 5 x 4		
Voice • The writer's personality is evident. • The writer shows feelings and emotions. • The reader feels connected to the writer and senses the humor, suspense, etc., in the writing.	1 2 3 4 5 x 3		
Word Choice • The words chosen are precise, active, and descriptive and create a clear mental picture. • Word choice is appropriate to the purpose and the audience.	1 2 3 4 5 x 3		
Sentence Fluency • The writing flows smoothly and naturally. • Sentence length and structure vary.	1 2 3 4 5 x 3		
Conventions • The writing follows standard capitalization, punctuation, spelling, and usage rules.	1 2 3 4 5 x 2		
Presentation • The paper is neat and legible. • The composition follows the correct format.	1 2 3 4 5 x 1		
TOTAL			

Analytic Writing Traits Scoring Overview Grid

For individual use, write the student's name on the line above and assignments in the boxes below. For group use, write the assignment at the top and students' names in the boxes below.

	Content	Organization	Voice	Word Choice	Fluency	Conventions	Presentation

Writing Process Checklist

For individual use, write the name on the line above and dates of observations between the slanted lines. For group use, write students' names between the slanted lines.

– = Beginning	√ = Developing
	√+ = Proficient

Prewriting					
Brainstorms possible topics					
Uses strategies to narrow topics					
Uses graphic organizers to plan writing					
Drafting					
Gets ideas down on paper					
Writes a complete first draft					
Revising					
Shares draft with others					
Clarifies ideas					
Adds details if necessary					
Reorganizes structure as necessary					
Revises sentences effectively					
Replaces weak words					
Proofreading					
Uses proofreading marks					
Identifies spelling, usage, and mechanics errors					
Makes necessary corrections					
Publishing					
Creates title					
Creates clean copy					
Shares work with others					

Comments: _____

_____

Integrated Theme Test Class Record

You may wish to write below or next to each category the specific skills covered by the theme test this chart represents.

E = Excellent

G = Good

S = Some Progress

N = Needs Improvement

Name	Reading Strategies	Comprehension/ Comparing Texts		Phonemic Awareness (K)	Phonics/Structural Analysis/Vocabulary	Writing and Language			Listening Comprehension	Self-Assessment
		Written	Multiple-Choice			Fluency	Language	Writing Skills		

Note: The Listening Comprehension subtest is optional and therefore not included in the score ranges listed in the Integrated Theme Test. If you choose to give the subtest, evaluate answers for evidence of strengths and weaknesses. Scoring of Self-Assessment is not recommended. Evaluate answers for evidence of metacognitive growth.

Theme Skills Test Class Record

Each test category contains one or more parts. Record the total score for each category. Check individual Student Record Forms of students with low scores for information on specific skill difficulties.

Name	Phonemic Awareness (K)	Phonics/Decoding/ Structural Analysis	High-Frequency Words	Comprehension Skills	Information and Study Skills	Spelling	Vocabulary	Grammar	Writing Skills

Test-Taking Strategies

General Strategies

- Get plenty of sleep and eat properly before the test. Take a watch with you.

- Relax! Use simple relaxation techniques when you feel nervous.

- Think positively. Concentrate on doing your best. Block out distractions.

- Listen to and/or read the test directions carefully. Ask questions if necessary.

- Feel free to mark up your test booklet.

- Pace yourself. Watch the time, but don't rush.

- If you don't know an answer, skip the question and go back to it later.

- Recheck answers you're unsure of. Change an answer only for a good reason.

- Fill out your answer sheet accurately and neatly.

- If you are answering questions based on a reading passage, read the questions first, and keep them in mind as you read the passage.

- Look for the answers in the passage. Don't rely only on what you know.

Answering Multiple-Choice Questions

- Read all answer choices before choosing the one you think is best.

- Eliminate answers you know are wrong; then make an educated guess.

- Watch for distracters—wrong answers that look right.

Answering Open-Response Questions About a Reading Passage

- Look for clues that tell the purpose and the topic of the question.

- Look in the passage for facts or other details that answer the question.

- Take notes, listing details and facts from the passage that help answer the question.

- Use keywords from the question in your answer.

- Support your answer with details and exact words from the passage. Repeat the details correctly.

- Use connecting words that support your purpose, such as to show cause and effect or time order.

- Write enough to answer the question, but don't write too much.

- Don't leave any question unanswered. Answer every one as well as you can.

- If a question has more than one part, answer all parts.

- Answer in complete sentences. Check spelling, punctuation, and capitalization.

- Use your best handwriting.

Writing to a Prompt

- Look for clue words in the prompt that tell the topic and the purpose of your composition.

- Brainstorm ideas on the topic, and make notes.

- Include all the key parts of a composition that fits the purpose in the prompt, such as to tell a story or to persuade.

English Language Learners Checklist (Kindergarten)

Student's Name _____

Theme/Selection _____

Language Proficiency Level   ☐ Beginning/Preproduction   ☐ Speech Emergent
                                   ☐ Early Production   ☐ Intermediate/Advanced

To evaluate student's progress, observe behaviors at different times. Use a plus (+) or a minus (–) symbol to indicate that the student has or has not successfully exhibited the behavior.

	Date	Date	Date	Comments
Beginning/Preproduction				
Comprehends simple repeated sentences				
Responds nonverbally, by gesturing and by imitating				
Follows simple 1- or 2-step directions				
Begins to chime in as class recites poems, songs, and chants				
Follows along during picture walks				
Uses illustrations and other graphic clues to comprehend printed material				
Illustrates to convey meaning				
Early Production				
Listens to and comprehends simple text				
Shows comprehension by using one or two words				
Begins to follow group discussions				
Chimes in during group reading of familiar text				
Makes short, appropriate oral responses to questions				
Uses everyday, basic vocabulary				
Uses pictures and/or simple symbols (heart, smiling face, x) to convey messages				
Conveys stories or simple ideas in drawings				
Uses pictures and objects to retell stories				
Uses pictures to complete sentence frames				
Begins to associate written text with spoken words				

English Language Learners Checklist (Kindergarten)

Student's Name _____

Theme/Selection _____

Language Proficiency Level ☐ Beginning/Preproduction   ☐ Speech Emergent
☐ Early Production   ☐ Intermediate/Advanced

To evaluate student's progress, observe behaviors at different times. Use a plus (+) or a minus (−) symbol to indicate that the student has or has not successfully exhibited the behavior.

	Date	Date	Date	Comments
Speech Emergent				
Understands what is said, with pauses				
Understands predictable read-alouds				
Follows a series of directions				
Uses context to supply missing words				
Takes part in discussions				
Engages in dialogues and role-plays				
Answers questions about characters				
Speaks in phrases or simple sentences				
Reads or recites simple, familiar texts				
Dictates simple labels or captions				
Matches printed words to some objects, people, actions				
Intermediate/Advanced				
Understands what is said with occasional repetition				
Comprehends stories and nonfiction selections at grade level				
Formulates and asks questions				
Expresses feelings and experiences				
Engages in nearly fluent conversation				
Dictates complete sentences				
Reads or recites familiar texts				
Answers questions about main ideas				
Uses compare and contrast, cause and effect				
Begins using decoding skills and context to read words				
Begins writing names of classmates and family members				

English Language Learners Checklist (Grades 1–2)

Student's Name _____

Theme/Selection _____

Language Proficiency Level ☐ Beginning/Preproduction   ☐ Speech Emergent
☐ Early Production   ☐ Intermediate/Advanced

To evaluate student's progress, observe behaviors at different times. Use a plus (+) or a minus (–) symbol to indicate that the student has or has not successfully exhibited the behavior.

	Date	Date	Date	Comments
Beginning/Preproduction				
Comprehends simple repeated sentences				
Responds nonverbally, by gesturing and by imitating				
Follows simple 1- or 2-step directions				
Begins to chime in as class recites poems, songs, and chants				
Follows along during picture walks				
Uses illustrations and other graphic clues to comprehend printed material				
Illustrates to convey meaning				
Begins to associate written text with spoken words				
Early Production				
Comprehends simple text				
Shows comprehension by using one or two words				
Begins to follow group discussions				
Makes short, appropriate oral responses to questions				
Uses everyday, basic vocabulary				
Uses rebuses and illustrations to convey ideas				
Uses pictures and objects to retell stories				
Follows text during group reading				
Matches written words to some objects, people, and actions				
Labels illustrations of objects, people, and actions				
Writes names and simple words				

English Language Learners Checklist (Grades 1–2)

Student's Name _____

Theme/Selection _____

Language Proficiency Level
☐ Beginning/Preproduction ☐ Speech Emergent
☐ Early Production ☐ Intermediate/Advanced

To evaluate student's progress, observe behaviors at different times. Use a plus (+) or a minus (–) symbol to indicate that the student has or has not successfully exhibited the behavior.

	Date	Date	Date	Comments
Speech Emergent				
Understands most of what is said with frequent pauses				
Comprehends stories read aloud				
Follows a series of directions				
Takes part in discussions				
Engages in dialogues and role-plays				
Speaks in phrases or simple sentences				
Reads aloud simple texts				
Uses decoding skills and context to read words				
Identifies characters				
Identifies main ideas				
Writes from dictation				
Writes simple sentences using details				
Completes sentence and story frames				
Intermediate/Advanced				
Understands what is said with occasional repetition				
Comprehends stories and nonfiction selections at grade level				
Formulates and asks questions				
Expresses feelings and experiences				
Begins to recognize idioms				
Paraphrases				
Engages in nearly fluent conversation				
Identifies story elements				
Reads aloud and silently				
Writes to describe, inform, persuade				
Uses correct grammar and mechanics				

English Language Learners Checklist (Grades 3–6)

Student's Name _____

Theme/Selection _____

Language Proficiency Level ☐ Beginning/Preproduction ☐ Speech Emergent
☐ Early Production ☐ Intermediate/Advanced

To evaluate student's progress, observe behaviors at different times. Use a plus (+) or a minus (–) symbol to indicate that the student has or has not successfully exhibited the behavior.

	Date	Date	Date	Comments
Beginning/Preproduction				
Comprehends simple repeated sentences				
Responds nonverbally, by gesturing and by imitating				
Follows simple 1- or 2-step directions				
Begins to chime in as class recites poems, songs, and chants				
Follows along during picture walks				
Uses illustrations and other graphic clues to comprehend printed material				
Illustrates to convey meaning				
Begins to associate written text with spoken words				
Early Production				
Comprehends simple text				
Shows comprehension by using one or two words				
Begins to follow group discussions				
Makes short, appropriate oral responses to questions				
Uses everyday, basic vocabulary				
Uses rebuses and illustrations to convey ideas				
Follows text during group reading				
Matches written words to some objects, people, and actions				
Labels illustrations of objects, people, and actions				
Writes names and simple words				
Attempts to write and spell unknown words				

English Language Learners Checklist (Grades 3–6)

....

Student's Name _____

Theme/Selection _____

Language Proficiency Level   ☐ Beginning/Preproduction   ☐ Speech Emergent
                                 ☐ Early Production   ☐ Intermediate/Advanced

To evaluate student's progress, observe behaviors at different times. Use a plus (+) or a minus (–) symbol to indicate that the student has or has not successfully exhibited the behavior.

	Date	Date	Date	Comments
Speech Emergent				
Understands most of what is said with frequent pauses				
Comprehends stories read aloud				
Follows a series of directions				
Takes part in discussions				
Engages in dialogues and role-plays				
Speaks in phrases or simple sentences				
Reads aloud simple texts				
Uses context and decoding skills				
Identifies characters				
Identifies main ideas				
Writes from dictation				
Writes simple sentences				
Uses details to complete sentence and story frames				
Intermediate/Advanced				
Understands what is said with occasional repetition				
Comprehends stories and nonfiction selections at grade level				
Formulates and asks questions				
Expresses feelings and experiences				
Begins to recognize idioms				
Paraphrases				
Engages in nearly fluent conversation				
Identifies story elements				
Reads aloud and silently				
Writes to describe, inform, persuade				
Incorporates new grammatical rules				
Uses correct grammar and mechanics				

Graph of Oral Fluency Growth

Student's Name _____

To evaluate growth in oral fluency, record the student's words correct per minute several times over a period of weeks or months. Note words correct per minute on the left of the graph and dates across the top. Scores can then be plotted and connected to show improvement over time.

Dates

Words Correct per Minute

0

Comments: _____

_____

Glossary

analytic scoring A scoring system that assesses individual elements of a piece of writing and assigns them numerical values.

anecdotal records Brief notes recording teacher observations of a student at work.

balanced assessment A blend of formal and informal assessment measures that includes a variety of authentic tasks and meaningful activities.

evaluation notebook A large three-ring notebook, with tabbed sections for each student, used to store tests, anecdotal notes, observation checklists, and other assessment data for the teacher's use.

formal assessment Teacher-made tests and published review tests, as well as state or district-mandated standardized tests.

holistic scoring A system that assesses how the different parts of a work, such as a piece of writing, work together as a whole.

ongoing informal assessment Assessment that focuses on process as well as product and includes ongoing observation of student behaviors and review of student work samples.

oral reading record A form of oral-reading analysis used to evaluate individual students' decoding and word-analysis skills and their use of reading strategies.

portfolio A collection of student work chosen by teacher and/or student to show progress and achievement over time.

portfolio slip A form used by a teacher or a student to indicate why a particular piece was chosen for the portfolio.

rubric A chart that shows the criteria by which student work will be evaluated; it may include a number score for each criterion or set of criteria.

scoring criteria The elements of an assignment that will be assessed to determine its score in a holistic or analytic scoring system.

self-assessment Evaluating one's own work or understanding of a concept, usually based on a set of criteria.

standards-based assessment Assessment that is based on specific content standards covering what students should know and be able to do.

Bibliography

Internet Sites

AskERIC (Educational Resources Information Center) is a federally funded national information system providing products and services on education issues, lesson plans, collections, a searchable database, and more; includes a link to the ERIC Clearinghouse on Assessment and Evaluation. **http://ericir.syr.edu/**

The Education Place home page links you to HOUGHTON MIFFLIN READING, professional resources, and other valuable Internet sites. **http://www.eduplace.com/rdg/**

Books and Articles

Andrade, H.G. (2000). Using rubrics to promote thinking and learning. *Educational Leadership,* 57, 13–18.

Barrentine, S.J. (Ed.) (1999). *Reading assessment: Principles and practices for elementary teachers. A collection of articles from "The Reading Teacher."* Newark, DE: International Reading Association.

Colby, S.A. (1999). Grading in a standards-based system. *Educational Leadership,* 56, 52–55.

Cooper, J.D. & Kiger, N.D. (2001). *Literacy Assessment; Helping teachers plan instruction.* Boston: Houghton Mifflin Company.

Falk, B. & Ort, S. (1998). Sitting down to score: Teacher learning through assessment. *Phi Delta Kappan,* 80, 59–64.

Mabry, L. (1999). Writing to the rubric: Lingering effects of traditional standardized testing on direct writing assessment. *Phi Delta Kappan,* 80, 673–679.

Schmoker, M. & Marzano, R.J. (1999). Realizing the promise of standards-based education. *Educational Leadership,* 56, 17–21.

Shepard, L. A. (1995). Using assessment to improve learning. *Educational Leadership,* 52, 38–43.

Skillings, M.J. & Ferrell, R. (2000). Student-generated rubrics: Bringing students into the assessment process. *The Reading Teacher,* 53, 452–455.

Valencia, S.W. (1998). *Literacy portfolios in action.* Belmont, CA: Wadsworth Publishing.

Wolf, D.P. & White, A.M. (2000). Charting the course of student growth. *Educational Leadership,* 57, 6–11.